T0195899

THE JOURNEY TO GREATNESS

JOHNSON F. ODESOLA

authorHOUSE®

AuthorHouse™
1663 Liberty Drive
Bloomington, IN 47403
www.authorhouse.com
Phone: 1 (800) 839-8640

Scripture taken from The Holy Bible, King James Version. Public Domain

Published by AuthorHouse 12/21/2019

ISBN: 978-1-7283-4085-2 (sc)
ISBN: 978-1-7283-4084-5 (e)

CONTENTS

CHAPTER
ONE

➡️

GREATNESS:
YOUR HERITAGE

The word GREAT means very big, large scale, very good; important; superior or admirable. It means more than ordinary; commanding and exceptional. The direct opposite of it is little. There are people who are little. In the order of strength, there are:

Little people
Average people
Great people

Greatness is the condition of being endowed with extraordinary power, uncommonly gifted; being able to accomplish vast results. It also depicts strength, influence, nobility. Greatness can also be an appellation. Have you ever heard of Alexander the **Great**? Greatness speaks of a person of major significance, accomplishment or acclaim.

God is Great. He is greater than the greatest, stronger than the strongest, wiser than the wisest, bigger than the biggest and better than the best. I am particularly thrilled by the following lyric:

'you are great, yes you are, Holy One
You walked upon the sea, raised the dead
You reign in majesty, mighty God
Everything written about you is great

'You are great
Yes, you are great
You are great
You are great
Everything written about you is great!

One of the legends of history, William Shakespeare said:

'Be not afraid of greatness; some are born great, some achieve greatness and others have greatness thrust upon them'.

As blood bought and blood washed believers, we are born great. The second birth which is otherwise called regeneration is divine birth into greatness. Are you genuinely born again? You are born great! Greatness is inherent, implicit and intrinsic in you!

Like begets like. A cow cannot give birth to a goat. When you got born again, you got born of God. God is great, you cannot be little except by your permission. God is the Most High God. You cannot be a most low person if you are born of God and take up your legal rights.

It amazes me when a believer cringes and grovels at the feet of the defeated foe, the devil. You are sitting with Christ in the heavenly places, how can the devil still be able to sit on you to torment you? Light is superior to darkness any moment. Can the dog chase a lion? Satan is the dog! You are the lion! Stand up and take your place in the redemptive package of Christ.

You are great. Talk to yourself that you are. If you do not acknowledge the fact that you are great, you may never be able to actualize this reality. You are an original and not a copy. You are the head and not the tail. You are above and not beneath. You are great and not little!

If you look into the mirror, you will find the most elegant person on earth. You are! Stop this wishy-washy life of mediocrity. Greatness is your heritage. You cannot be ordinary when your Maker is extraordinary. There is a seed of greatness in you.

'You were designed for accomplishment, engineered for success, and endowed with the seeds of greatness'- Zig Ziglar

'God has planted greatness in you. Let today be the beginning of a great adventure as you step into the gifts He's given you'- Joyce Meryer

Jesus, by His sacrifice on the cross paid for our greatness. This may be a surprise to many people who do not know that God has already programmed us to be great. There is a deposit of greatness in you, no matter how little you look in your eyes or in the eyes of other people.

'For since by man came death, by man came also the resurrection of the dead. For as in Adam all die, even so in Christ shall all be made alive'- 1 Cor. 15:21-22

'But not as the offence, so also is the free gift. For if through the offence of one many be dead, much more the grace of God, and the gift by grace, which is by one man, Jesus Christ, hath abounded unto many. And not as it was by one that sinned, so is the gift: for the judgment was by one to condemnation, but the free gift is of many offences unto justification. For if by one man's offence death reigned by one; much more they which receive abundance of grace and of the gift of righteousness shall reign in life by one, Jesus Christ.) Therefore as by the offence of one judgment came upon all men to condemnation; even so by the righteousness of one the free gift came upon all men unto justification of life. For as by one man's disobedience many were made sinners, so by the obedience of one shall many be made righteous'- Rom. 5:15-19

What a great privilege we have as believers! Everything Adam lost through the fall at the Garden of Eden was reclaimed for us by the sacrifice of Jesus at Cavalry. Adam was a great man at creation until he lost his glory at Eden. God did not give names to the animals He created in that vast garden neither did He name the woman He created from the side of Adam. It was Adam's call. Drawing from his supernatural instinct and greatness within, he gave names to all he animals one after the other. His accurateness and exactitude is an evidence of the greatness within him. He manifested the greatness of God!

By His death and resurrection, Jesus restored that glory. He took our unrighteousness and gave us His righteousness. He took our poverty and gave us His prosperity. He took our littleness and gave us His greatness. Yes, Jesus took our ordinariness and infused us with His extra-ordinariness. We are great! We are kings and priests in Christ! We are winners and champions in Christ! Yea, we are more than conquerors through Christ!

'He that spared not his own Son, but delivered him up for us all, how shall he not with him also freely give us all things?'- Rom. 8:32

God did not spare His only begotten Son but freely gave Him for our redemption and restoration to the original great status. Jesus freely offered Himself too as sacrifice for our redemption and restoration. Now, if God could give His only begotten son to redeem us, do you think He will hold back tangible, transient and ephemeral things from us? He will freely give us all things. Indeed, He has freely given us all things!

'Charge them that are rich in this world, that they be not high-minded, nor trust in uncertain riches, but in the living God, who giveth us richly all things to enjoy'- 1 Tim. 6:17

God has given to us all things freely to enjoy. He has made us great. If you are not enjoying all things already provided by God, I have good news for you. This book will open you up to your rights and privileges in Christ, reveal certain principles you need to apply to access the greatness of God and help you to become actually great if you will be willing and obedient to obey instructions.

God blessed Abraham above and beyond human comprehension. Abraham carried the aura of greatness. He was a carrier of the blessing of God. When we talk of all round greatness, Abraham readily comes to mind. He is a perfect example of a great man. It may interest you to know that all the blessings of Abraham are now available for us through Christ Jesus. That is, in Christ, we possess all and more of the Abrahamic blessings.

'Christ hath redeemed us from the curse of the law, being made a curse for us: for it is written, Cursed is every one that hangeth on a tree: That the blessing of Abraham might come on the Gentiles through Jesus Christ; that we might receive the promise of the Spirit through faith'- Gal. 3:13-14.

Abraham was a great man! He was great spiritually, materially and otherwise. Let me make it very clear to you right now that Abraham's blessings are yours! Believe it. If you believe it and obey the instructions you will be given in this book, you will receive all blessings God has provided for you. God blessed the nations of the world through Abraham. When He called Abraham to get out of his country to a place He would lead him, He promised to bless the nations on earth through him. He has since fulfilled His promise.

'Now the LORD had said unto Abram, Get thee out of thy country, and from thy kindred, and from thy father's house, unto a land that I will show thee: And I will make of thee a great nation, and I will bless thee, and make thy name great; and thou shalt be a blessing'- Gen.12:1-2

He blessed the nations of the world through Abraham. Now, He has blessed us in Christ Jesus. When a poor village girl gets married

5

to a rich and great city billionaire, her poverty and littleness will disappear into thin air. All her needs will be met as long as she remains the bride of the rich and great man. In the real sense, she is no longer poor or little. By virtue of her marital affiliation, she is a rich and great woman! Her children will be rich and great too!

'The Spirit itself beareth witness with our spirit, that we are the children of God: And if children, then heirs; heirs of God, and joint-heirs with Christ...'- Rom. 8:16-17

'And because ye are sons, God hath sent forth the Spirit of his Son into your hearts, crying, Abba, Father. Wherefore thou art no more a servant, but a son; and if a son, then an heir of God through Christ'- Gal. 4:6-7

Jesus is the Heir of all things in heaven and earth. The Bible says we are joint heirs with Him. We are heirs of God through Christ! What is the right and privilege of an heir? Inheritance, the heir is to inherit all things his father possesses. Jesus is in total control of all things our Father has. We are joint heirs with Him, so we are designed to inherit all things with Him! We are designed and destined to be great with Him!

Get out of that grasshopper mentality complex! You are great. If you are little in your eyes, you will be little in the eyes of other people. Get ready to manifest the greatness of God in you. Get ready to manifest the glory of God as sons and heirs through Christ! Get ready to make God proud! God is proud when we actually exhibit His greatness. He can proudly tell satan, 'that's my son! That's my daughter! That was how He was proud of a great man called Job. May God be proud of you too!

It doesn't matter your present situation, you can still manifest the greatness of God locked up within you. I have written a book titled UNLOCKING YOUR DESTINY. You will do well to have a copy.

By virtue of the authority of Jesus vested in me, I speak concerning your life right now:

- You will blaze forth from obscurity into meteoric prominence in Jesus name!
- You will be celebrated and not tolerated in Jesus name!
- You will manifest the greatness and glory of God!
- Your mess will become a message in this messed age!
- Your siege will be over and a new dawn of abundance will hit you.
- You will sing a new song: the song of greatness.
- Your insults will be turned to results, your shame to fame and your story to glory.
- Your tests will become testimony, your tears will turn to treasure, your obstacles to miracles and your stumbling blocks to stepping stones in the mighty name of Jesus!

CHAPTER
TWO

➡️

WHEN YOU WAKE UP TO REALITY

'Then Elisha said, Hear ye the word of the LORD; Thus saith the LORD, Tomorrow about this time shall a measure of fine flour be sold for a shekel, and two measures of barley for a shekel, in the gate of Samaria. Then a lord on whose hand the king leaned answered the man of God, and said, Behold, if the LORD would make windows in heaven, might this thing be? And he said, Behold, thou shalt see it with thine eyes, but shalt not eat thereof. And there were four leprous men at the entering in of the gate: and they said one to another, Why sit we here until we die?'- 2 kings 7:1-3

Samaria was under siege by Syria. It was a protracted siege that brought a great famine. Economic activities were halted. The famine became so severe that children were killed, cooked and eaten like beef. It was pathetic! It was bizarre! In the midst of this hopeless and helpless situation, Elisha proclaimed abundance.

When God speaks, it is settled. His word is potent and infallible. God begins when man gets to his wit's end. Man's bus stop is God's starting point. When hope is lost, God is always the last resort. Irreversible situations are reversible with God. He terminates terminal ailments.

He is the hope of the hopeless and help of the helpless. With Him, all things are possible. He performs His promises. He wipes away tears and brings laughter in place. He limits limitations, hinder hindrances and bar barriers. With God, there are no limits.

In a regular video player, there is usually a **stop button, pause button** and **play button**. When a woman gets to a certain age, people call it **menopause**. They say she can no longer conceive and deliver a baby. Where there is **'menopause'**, there is **'menoplay'** with God. Menopause is not really the end to child bearing. With God, there is menoplay. On the journey to greatness, you are unstoppable if you are ready and willing to wake up to reality.

FOUR LEPERS BECAME HEROES

'And there were four leprous men at the entering in of the gate: and they said one to another, Why sit we here until we die? If we say, We will enter into the city, then the famine is in the city, and we shall die there: and if we sit still here, we die also. Now therefore come, and let us fall unto the host of the Syrians: if they save us alive, we shall live; and if they kill us, we shall but die. And they rose up in the twilight, to go unto the camp of the Syrians: and when they were come to the uttermost part of the camp of Syria, behold, there was no man there'- 2 Kings 7:3-5

They lived in the suburb of the city in their colony. The famine that ravaged the entire county as a result of the Syrian siege had a toll on them too. This day, they sat at the gate in penury, hunger and thirst. Their predicament was not different from those who dwelt in the metropolis. At least, two families had agreed to kill, cook and eat their children in turn. This carnivorous experience had just started when the king heard. Elisha was handy. He proclaimed abundance.

At the gate of the city, the four little, mere, ordinary men woke up to reality. It occurred to them that they had the chance to either live or die; to either remain little or become great; to either perish in

9

poverty or live in affluence. By survival instinct, they rose up and embarked on the journey; *the journey to greatness.*

'And when these lepers came to the uttermost part of the camp, they went into one tent, and did eat and drink, and carried thence silver, and gold, and raiment, and went and hid it; and came again, and entered into another tent, and carried thence also, and went and hid it'- 2 Kings 7:8.

At the gate, in their littleness and ordinariness, they faced a biting hunger. Now, their journey to greatness had brought them abundance of food and drink. They ate and drank to satisfaction. They were blessed with silver, gold and raiment. Their status had changed! It was going to change further and they were going to become heroes.

'So they came and called unto the porter of the city: and they told them, saying, We came to the camp of the Syrians, and, behold, there was no man there, neither voice of man, but horses tied, and asses tied, and the tents as they were. And he called the porters; and they told it to the king's house within.'- 2 Kings 7:10-11

They carried the message of abundance to the king. Whereas they were messengers of lack, emptiness and poverty, they were now messengers of plenty, greatness and hope. They were carriers of greatness and bearers of good tidings. They became heroes within the twenty four hours window that abundance was proclaimed by the prophet of God. **The prophet of God only knew and proclaimed by faith that there will be abundance. It was these four lepers that led the way to the abundance.**

In what areas of your life do you seek a drastic turn around? Are you down by overwhelming circumstances of life? Are you in a dale of confusion? Do you think there is no hope anymore? Do you think it is too late to become great in life? Does the future look bleak and black? Is it dark and dreary? Are you clutched and clamped down with fear of tomorrow? Are there terminal issues around you? Are you facing real storms of life?

I am glad to inform you here that you can ascend the ladder of greatness in life. You can overcome your obstacles, mount your mountains and hinder your hindrances. Yes, you can limit your limitations and blaze forth from obscurity into meteoric prominence. When you are ready to wake up to the reality of all round victory in life, you will experience the following:

Your lack will turn to abundance

Look at the sudden, dramatic and drastic change that the four lepers experienced within twenty four hours! Their status changed from **four lepers** to **four heroes**. In twenty four hours, the Samarian famine was turned to abundance. The siege was suddenly over.

Oh, I hear the sound of abundance around your corner. I see the cloud gathering to release the rains of abundance. Do you believe you can rise to the top? All things are possible to those who believe! Greatness is achievable.

The widow of the prophet who passed on to glory was in a precarious and pathetic situation. Her source of joy was suddenly cut short. As if her predicament was not bad enough, she inherited huge debt that threatened her family unity. She was about to lose her two sons to the creditor. Her story changed when she woke up to reality and leveraged on the anointed man of God. She was optimistic there was solution to her predicament. That was why she sought for help from the man of God. Her approach rolled away her reproach

'I have been young, and now am old; yet have I not seen the righteous forsaken, nor his seed begging bread'- Psalms 37:25

David was a great man by any standard and in all ramifications. His submission that God does not forsake the downtrodden holds water. He was an evidence of progress from obscurity to meteoric prominence. He was an ordinary shepherd boy who rose to the throne as shepherd of Israel. The seed of greatness in him began to manifest when he defended the flock from predators in jeopardy of his life. It became obvious in the battle field when he mowed down Goliath of Gath like tender mushroom. The anointing of God had touched his head. He was unstoppable in the journey to greatness.

The anointing of God is upon you as a believer in Christ. You are anointed to be great. You are anointed to be successful. Your second birth in Christ was birth into greatness. Be unstoppable! Wake up to this reality!

'But the anointing which ye have received of him abideth in you, and ye need not that any man teach you: but as the same anointing teacheth you of all things, and is truth, and is no lie, and even as it hath taught you, ye shall abide in him'- 1 John 2:27

Your stagnancy will turn to unstoppable progress

Blind Bartimaeus had several odds against him. He was blind, poor and hopeless. For several years, he remained little and ordinary in the eyes of people from whom he received handouts. He was in this condition until he woke up to the reality that his condition could change. Jesus was ministering along the way he usually sat to beg.

'And when he heard that it was Jesus of Nazareth, he began to cry out, and say, Jesus, thou son of David, have mercy on me- Mark 10:47

Bartimaeus cried out to Jesus to change his predicament. He had sat for several years begging for alms. Now, he desired to be a giver and not only a receiver. He desired to see, live a normal life and be more useful to the society. He desired to be great too! Nothing would deter him now. He had begged for alms enough. His earnest desire was a drastic and dramatic turn-around.

'And many charged him that he should hold his peace...' —Mark 10:48a

When you wake up to the reality of the inherent greatness in you, you will become irresistible and unstoppable. A crowd of opposition resisted the earnest desire of blind Bartimaeus. They shouted at him to keep quiet. By the estimate of these people who have constituted themselves as obstacle, blind Bartimaeus was not worth anything. He was too little, mean and mere. He was too ordinary.

'...but he cried the more a great deal, Thou son of David, have mercy on me'- Mark 10:48b

They shouted at him to keep quiet but his voice overwhelmed their voices. He had been stagnant for so long. Now, he would be unstoppable. He would make meaningful progress. Rather than keep mum, he shouted the more. His voice reached the rooftop. Tired of sitting at the road side as a mere beggar, he was ready to move up the ladder and become a giver. He was ready to become actually great.

'And he, casting away his garment, rose, and came to Jesus'- Mark 10:50

Jesus stood still for him. He stood still to give him his much needed attention. Blind Bartimaeus maximized the golden opportunity. He made haste, cast away his garment and meandered his way through the crowd to meet Jesus. His stagnancy was turned to unstoppable progress.

When you wake up to the reality of your inherent greatness, you will become unstoppable. There was a certain woman who suffered for twelve years without progress in her health. She was stagnant in her state of health. Rather than improve, her health deteriorated until she woke up to the reality that she could live in health. She had wasted all her savings to get well.

A twelve year period is long enough to achieve great things. You can get married and bear children within a period of twelve years.

You can go to school and become a doctor, engineer, lawyer etc, within a period of twelve years. You can buy cars, build houses, travel overseas, establish a business, etc within a period of twelve years!

'When she had heard of Jesus, came in the press behind, and touched his garment'- Mark 5:27

This woman was enmeshed in the stormy waters of ill health for twelve years. She wallowed in this misery until the day she woke up to take her destiny in her hands. Her journey to health began from her position behind the crowd that thronged Jesus. She meandered through until she got to the Greater than the greatest. She was unstoppable. Her healing was unstoppable too.

'And Jabez was more honourable than his brethren: and his mother called his name Jabez, saying, because I bare him with sorrow. And Jabez called on the God of Israel, saying, Oh that thou wouldest bless me indeed, and enlarge my coast, and that thine hand might be with me, and that thou wouldest keep me from evil, that it may not grieve me! And God granted him that which he requested'- 1Chron. 4:9-10

Jabez was fed up with his miserable condition. He was a son of sorrow, born into sorrow and he lived in this sorrowful condition until he decided to look up and hook up to the God of greatness. He knew there was more to life than his wishy-washy low life. He knew there is something better than his prevailing condition. He knew he could live a better life, make meaningful progress and be a channel of blessing. That was exactly what he got. He became great according to his desire.

It doesn't matter how long you have been in your present ordinary, mere and low-rated condition. You can be great. You can experience 180 degree turn around. You can be celebrated. You can attain enviable heights of valour. It all depends on your decision today to wake up to the reality of your inherent greatness.

Your hope will be revived

The story of a Moabitess, Ruth readily strikes the mind when we talk about the journey to greatness. She was a young damsel thrown in a dale of confusion in her prime age when she should enjoy her marriage to a noble man. She was bereaved of her husband and father in-law. Left childless and a widow, she faced the challenge of spiritual, emotional and economic survival. Her plight depicted emptiness in all ramifications: childless, widowed, no father in-law, bereaved mother in-law, jobless and spiritually impoverished. Her only source of spiritual strength was Naomi, her mother in-law. Remember Moab was idolatry.

'And Ruth said, Entreat me not to leave thee, or to return from following after thee: for whither thou goest, I will go; and where thou lodgest, I will lodge: thy people shall be my people, and thy God my God: Where thou diest, will I die, and there will I be buried: the LORD do so to me, and more also, if ought but death part thee and me. When she saw that she was stedfastly minded to go with her, then she left speaking unto her'- Ruth 1:16-18

This poor childless widow decided to take a journey to greatness. First, she renounced idolatry and her pagan people. She chose the God and people of Naomi. From Moab, her land of nativity, she took a giant stride and embarked on the journey to greatness in Bethlehem-Judah. And she was resolute! Nothing would deter her. Nothing would discourage her in this desire for greatness.

Poverty often obscures the lustre of virtue. Now in a strange land, Bethlehem-Judah, this virtuous woman maintained a decent lifestyle. She was an epitome of good moral values and virtue. Instead of poverty to obscure the lustre of her virtue, her virtue took away the reproach of poverty. She did not let down her moral guards in spite of her emotional loneliness. Events after events played out until she got married to a noble man, Boaz and gave birth to Obed. The genealogy continued from Obed to Jesse, David, Solomon until

Christ! In the genealogy of our Lord and Saviour, Jesus Christ, Ruth was prominently mentioned. She blazed forth from obscurity to meteoric prominence.

In Ezekiel's valley of dry bones, the prevailing hopelessness that starred at the prophet was inconceivable. The bones were very dry; dead as dodo and scattered around the valley. The prophet confessed he had no idea whether the dry bones could ever live.

'The hand of the LORD was upon me, and carried me out in the spirit of the LORD, and set me down in the midst of the valley which was full of bones, And caused me to pass by them round about: and, behold, there were very many in the open valley; and, lo, they were very dry. And he said unto me, Son of man, can these bones live? And I answered, O Lord GOD, thou knowest'- Eze. 37:1-3

This was really a hopeless situation. Ezekiel prophesied as instructed. By his prophecy, he set in motion the journey to greatness. The dead and dry bones responded to the anointing. There is a prophetic dimension to greatness. The onus lies with you to obey instructions. The bones aligned; bone to bone, socket to socket and sinew to sinew.

'So I prophesied as I was commanded: and as I prophesied, there was a noise, and behold a shaking, and the bones came together, bone to his bone'- Eze. 37:7

Progressively, subsequent prophetic declarations were made. Hope was rising; light was emanating and greatness was in the offing. It was beginning to dawn on the prophet that indeed, there was hope in hopeless situations.

'Then said he unto me, Prophesy unto the wind, prophesy, son of man, and say to the wind, Thus saith the Lord GOD; Come from the four winds, O breath, and breathe upon these slain, that they may live. So I prophesied as

he commanded me, and the breath came into them, and they lived, and stood up upon their feet, an exceeding great army'- Eze. 37:9-10

Ezekiel prophesied again as commanded. Bang! It happened, breath came into the lifeless bodies and they lived. The Bible describes it as an exceeding great army. The deserted dry bones in the valley became a great army. This illustration is true of believers today. Are you at the bottom, weighed down by overwhelming circumstances of life? There is hope. Dry bones can live again. You can be great while you are alive!

Your dryness will be over

'And Elijah said unto Ahab, Get thee up, eat and drink; for there is a sound of abundance of rain'- 1 Kings 18:41

A single rain of abundance will cancel all your period of dryness. It happened in the days of Prophet Elijah. The draught that prevailed in the land was inconceivable. For three and half years, there was neither rain nor dew. The ensuing famine that engulfed the land was unprecedented. Dryness prevailed in no small measure. Brooks and other sources of water dried up. The vegetation was dry. This dryness was obvious in animals and in the inhabitants of the land.

Are there areas you are experiencing dryness? Is it spiritual lethargy and stupor? Is it in your marital relationship? In business or health? You can experience greatness in place of dryness. A single abundant rain exterminated protracted dryness and ushered in freshness. This is what will happen to you when you wake up to the reality of the greatness God desires for you. You will be great. You are great!

Your enemies will be stampeded out of your way

On your way to greatness, you will meet obstacles and oppositions. It is inevitable. In spite of this fact, I want you to understand that you are covered by the Greater than the greatest. The Almighty God has promised in His word to shield you from known and unknown enemies. They will be frustrated out of your way.

'What shall we then say to these things? If God be for us, who can be against us?'- Rom. 8:31

You will overcome your obstacles because **you are stronger than your enemies.** As they come against you in one way, they shall flee in seven ways. That was what happened in Syria. The enemies of Israel who had laid siege for an interminable length of time were stampeded out of the way for Israel to experience the abundance Prophet Elisha proclaimed.

'And Moses said unto the people, Fear ye not, stand still, and see the salvation of the LORD, which he will show to you today: for the Egyptians whom ye have seen today, ye shall see them again no more for ever. The LORD shall fight for you, and ye shall hold your peace'- Exo. 14:13-14

Moses and the children of Israel were sandwiched between two great enemies: Pharaoh's militia and the red sea. It was a hopeless situation. They were stagnated: couldn't go forward or backward. Total annihilation was in the offing. Rather than fall for the enemies, they looked up and hooked up. God miraculously led His children through the red sea and drowned the enemies in the red sea.

The onus is with you to wake up to the reality of greatness and make a concrete decision to go forward in life and ministry. Once you have made up your mind and you are willing to put the right pegs in the right holes, you will surmount insurmountable mountains, break through barriers and bring down impregnable walls because **you are stronger than your enemies.**

You will become a testimony

It is not enough to have testimony once in a while. This spasmodic experience of great things is not enough! It is like having drizzles when you can have showers of rain. It is like having showers when you can have torrents of rain. Torrent of blessings is God's earnest desire for you. You can be immersed in the waters of His greatness.

Wake up to this reality! You will not only have testimony but you will become a testimony. You will become a cynosure; an epitome of greatness. When people talk about greatness, you will readily become a reference point. You can be great for greater is He that is in you than he that is in the world.

Your shame will turn to fame

'And the LORD said unto Joshua, This day have I rolled away the reproach of Egypt from off you. Wherefore the name of the place is called Gilgal unto this day'- Joshua 5:9

Your approach will roll away your reproach. This is one truth you must grasp if you will climb the ladder of greatness in life. God has repeatedly turned shame to fame. A few examples of people who had their shame turned to fame include the following:

Zacchaeus: He was a notorious fraudster who brought disrepute to himself as a result of his nefarious activities. In the eyes of people, shame was his emblem. That was why they wondered that Jesus could associate with such ignoble personality. When Jesus finished with him, his shame was turned to fame. In the hall of those that had an enduring and fruitful encounter with Jesus, Zacchaeus name will always be mentioned.

The lame man at the beautiful gate: He sat daily at the gate of the temple to beg for alms. He survived on hand outs from generous worshippers. His shame was obvious to all and sundry. This special day, his story changed. Rather than sit at the gate in shame to beg, he leaped up on his feet and entered the temple with other worshippers. His shame was over. Now, he could walk and run. He could enter in and out of the temple to worship. He no longer needed to be carried about by other people. As his shame was obvious to people, his fame was noticed by everyone who knew him before.

Those who despised you before will honour you in no distant time as you embark on the journey to greatness in Jesus name! You will be accepted where you were rejected. You will have a YES where you had a NO. Those who saw you down there will see you up there. Your glory will not be subdued and your destiny will not be truncated in the precious name of Jesus!

Blind Bartimaeus: He too was a beggar. He sat by the highway every morning when other people go about their work or businesses. He survived only on their generosity. His life was characterized by shame: shame of being blind; shame of being a beggar: shame of being jobless: shame of being always alone and shame of being irrelevant to the society.

What is your shame? What stigma is hanging around you? You will move out of the terrain of shame to the realm of fame in the mighty name of Jesus! Blind Bartimaeus got over his shame. You will get over your shame in Jesus name!

The man born blind: His shame started from the day he was born. He came out of the womb blind! That was how he grew up until he became a full-fledged man. He did not have the privilege of education neither did he have an idea of what human beings, animals and the society he lived looked like. One word depicted his predicament: *shame.*

Jesus with His disciples saw him that fateful day. It was time for him to walk out on shame into the warm embrace of fame. Jesus does not give shame; it is Satan that distributes shame like gift. Jesus gives fame. This blind man who had his eyes opened became so famous that he was an object of discussion.

'The neighbours therefore, and they which before had seen him that he was blind, said, Is not this he that sat and begged? Some said, This is he: others said, He is like him: but he said, I am he'- John 9:8-9

The dramatic and sudden change of status amazed those who knew him. While some people believed he wasn't the same blind man they knew from birth, others said it was him. His shame had been turned to fame. He could now live as a normal human being like other people.

The woman with the issue of blood: She had an interrupted menstrual flow for twelve years! Her shame was unabated even after several medical consultations. She was an eyesore; an object of ridicule and an emblem of shame.

This pathetic woman became famous for her faith when she encountered Jesus, the giver of fame. The fountain of her flow ceased when she touched the helm of His garment. Jesus commended her faith. In place of shame, which she experienced for twelve years, she had fame.

Time and space will fail me to talk about various others who had their shame replaced with fame. The endless list includes the impotent man at the pool Bethesda, Saul of Tarsus, the syrophoenician woman whose daughter was daily tormented by demons, the widow of Nain who only son was raised from the casket, barren women who had notable children and several others too numerous to mention. You are next on the list. You are getting out of the list of shame in Jesus famous name!

CHAPTER
THREE

→

THE HALL OF GREATNESS

The Bible is dotted with great men and women who became great because they embarked on the journey to greatness. I will mention a few of them in this chapter. The lesson I want you to pick from this chapter is that you too can climb up the ladder of greatness.

Joseph was a great man

From a boy of a coat of many colours, he rose steadily to stardom. His journey to greatness began when he started out as a dreamer. He dreamt of greatness which was transmuted into reality several years later.

'And he said unto them, Hear, I pray you, this dream which I have dreamed: For, behold, we were binding sheaves in the field, and, lo, my sheaf arose, and also stood upright; and, behold, your sheaves stood round about, and made obeisance to my sheaf'- Gen. 37:6-7

'And he dreamed yet another dream, and told it his brethren, and said, Behold, I have dreamed a dream more; and, behold, the sun and the moon and the eleven stars made obeisance to me'- Gen. 37:9

The journey was rough and tough but in the long run, Joseph ascended the throne of greatness. It didn't look like he was going to succeed in life as events unfolded retrogressively. First, he was hated by his brethren who cast aspersion on him as a mere dreamer.

Joseph was introduced to the boot camp of rough and tough times early in life. At the age of seventeen, he was separated from his father. He had lofty dreams but he would go through the undulating path to greatness. He would climb up the ladder of greatness amidst forces of opposition.

His dilemma started when his father sent him to check out his siblings in the field where they went to feed the flock. This was the beginning of his journey to greatness. He had dreamt of greatness. His coat of many colours was certainly symbolic of his future greatness.

His brothers sighted him from afar and immediately plotted to kill him. They loathed his dreams of greatness. They had earlier questioned his guts and dreams of greatness that would place him above them. Now, this dreamer would not reign as long as they lived. He could reign but only in the dreamland. They would not want him reign in reality.

'And when they saw him afar off, even before he came near unto them, they conspired against him to slay him. And they said one to another, behold this dreamer cometh. Come now therefore, and let us slay him, and cast him into some pit, and we would say, some evil beast hath devoured him: and we shall see what will become of him'- Gen. 37:18-20

Joseph was a target of a murderous plot because he had lofty dreams. Do you have a lofty vision? Do you have a dream or desire to be great in life? This is what is required to attract hate and jealousy. If you desire to be great and practically take steps to be, you will become an object of hate. The devil will hate you with passion. He would do anything to stop you from becoming great.

Have a vision: you will become a target of hate. The enemy does not attack people who are going nowhere. You have many troubles because you are going somewhere to happen. You carry the blessing of God; the inherent greatness of God that is designed to touch several lives and bring out the best in them.

Joseph drew near the gangster that is supposed to cater for him as siblings. Rather can embrace him and his lofty dreams, they were full of jealousy and hate. Joe got punished for aspiring to be great. He was lowered into the pit after he was stripped of his coat of many colours. This was the suggestion of Reuben in lieu of their sinister and murderous plot.

'And Reuben said unto them, shed no blood, but cast him into this pit that is in the wilderness... And it came to pass, when Joseph was come unto his brethren, that they stripped Joseph out of his coat, his coat of many colours that was on him. And they took him and cast him into a pit...'- Gen. 37:22-24

Joseph was lowered into the pit. In the pit, he kept his dream alive. He kept his eyes on the throne of greatness. Nothing would strip him of his inherent greatness. He could be stripped of his coat of many colours but nothing would tamper with his innate and intrinsic desire for greatness.

Beloved brethren, keep your dreams and visions alive. There is life beyond the pit. God was with Joseph in his pitiable condition. God is with you in all that you have been passing through. He has not forsaken or abandoned you. What is required of you is to be strong in the Lord and in the power of His might. Don't ever give up your desire for greatness.

Joseph was brought out of the pit and sold to the Medianite travellers who in turn sold him to Potiphar, an officer in Pharaoh's cabinet. In the house of Potiphar, Joseph was a slave. In slavery, he discharged his responsibilities as a king. He had the mentality of a king though he did the back bending and menial works. His innate greatness manifested in his outlook, charisma, disposition and activities until he was entrusted with the entire house of Potiphar.

In the process of time in his journey to greatness, Mrs Potiphar lusted after Joseph who respectfully turned down her immoral overtures. What would attract a successful woman to a slave? There was that irresistible glory and aura around Joseph that this woman wrongly interpreted. Instead of helping Joseph to fan the amber of his greatness, she desired to satisfy the lust of her flesh. Her inordinate and immoral desire escalated until she falsely accused Joseph of attempting to rape her. Consequently, Joseph was incarcerated. He was unjustly incarcerated for standing for righteousness. He was unjustly incarcerated for refusing to be immoral. He was imprisoned for running away from evil.

Have you been in this situation? Have you been unjustly treated for standing for the truth? Has your good been evil spoken of? Have you been a victim of jealousy and hate? You are not alone in this ordeal my friend. Joseph was there. He went to jail simply because he wanted to live right. He desired to be great and one of the steps in the ladder of greatness is righteousness.

In the prison, Joseph kept his hope alive. Rather than sink in defeat, his anointing increased. Every ordeal, whether positive or negative pushed him up the ladder of greatness. Whereas he was only a dreamer when he was in his father's house, he could interpret dreams now. He narrated his dreams to his father for interpretation because he could not interpret dreams. Now people narrated their dreams to him for interpretation because he could now interpret dreams. Once a dreamer, now an interpreter of dreams. He interpreted the dreams of the chief baker and chief butler. Three days later, his interpretation was fulfilled. The baker was hung and the butler was released to his butlership. The butler forgot to speak well of him to Pharaoh.

'Yet did not the chief butler remember Joseph but forget him'- Gen. 40:23

Does it amaze you that people easily forget your good works instead of making you a reference point? Do you get negative rewards for your good works? Do people only give verbal appreciation for your great inputs? Do not let this depress you further. It is the attitude of men to remember the evil and forget the good a person does. Jesus healed ten lepers. Only one remembered to come back to appreciate him.

The chief butler whose dream Joseph interpreted forgot to speak well of Joseph to king Pharaoh. The sun cannot be stopped from rising in the East and setting in the West. When it is time for it to blaze forth, nothing can hinder it. When it is time for you to blaze forth into greatness, nothing can hinder you. Though he was forgotten in the prison, his greatness could not be restricted. He was great in the prison for he was made the head of the inmates. And from the prison, his greatness brought him to the palace.

'And Joseph was thirty years old when he stood before Pharaoh king of Egypt. And Joseph went out from the presence of Pharaoh, and went throughout all the land of Egypt'- Gen. 41:46

Joseph was thirty years old when he was brought before Pharaoh. He was only seventeen when he was snatched away from his father. For thirteen years, he wallowed in slavery and adversity upon adversity. Those thirteen years were not pleasant moments. He lived in pain and rejection until God remembered him. It is your time to be remembered. It is your turn to be celebrated.

In those days, there was a great famine all over the earth. There was only one place that had plenty of food and wine: the government house of Egypt where Joseph reigned as prime minister. He was appointed second in command after Pharaoh when he interpreted Pharaoh's dream.

'And Pharaoh said unto his servants, Can we find such a one as this is, a man in whom the Spirit of God is? And Pharaoh said unto Joseph, Forasmuch as God hath showed thee all this, there is none so discreet and wise as thou art: Thou shalt be over my house, and according unto thy word shall all my people be ruled: only in the throne will I be greater than thou'- Gen. 41:38-40

Pharaoh too saw the greatness in Joseph like Potiphar's wife saw. He went further to fan the amber of his greatness. He created a non-existent position in the country and gave Joseph the portfolio. Before Joseph, there was no position as Prime Minister. That is what will happen when your greatness breaks forth.

Now, the whole world was in hunger. There was no food except in Egypt. Jacob's household had exhausted their stock of food. This is in spite of the fact that Jacob was a very wealthy man. The Bible describes him as a man who increased exceedingly, and had much cattle, and maidservants, and menservants, and camels, and asses (Gen. 30:43)

'And the sons of Israel came to buy corn among those that came: for the famine was in the land of Canaan. And Joseph was the governor over the land, and he it was that sold to all the people of the land: and Joseph's brethren came, and bowed themselves before him with their faces to the earth. And Joseph saw his brethren and knew them, but made himself strange unto them....And Joseph knew his brethren but they knew him not'-Gen. 42:5-8

The famine that pervaded all over the earth, including Canaan was severe that the sons of Jacob had to resort to travel to Egypt to buy food. They came face to face with the man they maltreated and sold into slavery. As a matter of fact, they bowed their faces to the earth in obeisance. By now, something was becoming of his dream. He had dreamt that his brothers' sheaves bowed down to his sheaf that stood erect when he was seventeen. In order to stop the fulfilment of his dream, they had sold him to slavery. They said: *' ...and we shall see what will become of his dreams'*- Gen. 37:20

Don't give up your dreams. Keep the fire burning within you. At the appointed time, your difficult moments will to bow before you. Your littleness will bow to your greatness. Your adversity will bow down to your prosperity. You will see the fulfilment of your dreams.

'And Joseph knew his brethren but they knew him not'-Gen. 42:8

Joseph recognized his brethren but they couldn't recognize him. This is significant! He recognized them. They had not changed much. They had not improved in their physical appearance, dressing, disposition, educational standard, social status and ethics. There was no significant progress about them.

They couldn't recognize Joseph. He had drastically changed. His physical appearance had changed. His social status had changed too. The aura and glory around him was different. His personality had improved. He was no longer a mere dreamer but an interpreter of dreams and the governor of the land. He had made tremendous and significant progress in life. He had ascended the throne of greatness!

You can pick the following virtues from the life of this great man called Joseph:

1. He had integrity
2. He was faithful
3. He feared God
4. He was holy
5. He was patient
6. He was humble
7. He was selfless
8. He was morally sound
9. He was merciful and gracious

Abraham was a great man

Let me give you a quick synopsis of this great man of God before I zero briefly on his journey to greatness:

- He gave up his native land in obedience to God: Gen.12:1
- He trusted God for a child at old age: Romans 4:18-19
- He offered his only son to God: Gen.22:1-19

Abraham obeyed God by faith even though:

- ✓ He did not know *Where*
- ✓ He did not know *What*
- ✓ He did not know *How*
- ✓ He did not know *When*
- ✓ He did not know *Why*

Abraham was greatness personified. When you talk of great men, he readily comes to mind. He was an icon of faith, a symbol of fatherhood and a friend of God. His life and ministry is a reference point to us today. *'Abraham's blessings are mine'*. We quite quickly identify with his greatness.

In Genesis chapter 12, there was a severe famine but in chapter 13, Abraham was very rich. When there was a casting down, there was a lifting up for Abraham. Instead of going down in the season of famine, God made him stupendously rich. Instead of wallowing in debt, God made him abundantly wealthy.

'And Abram was very rich in cattle, in silver and in gold'- Gen. 13:2

When it is tough and rough, only great men will stand tall in defiance. Great men will always outlive difficult moments. Don't give up dearly beloved. You will get up if you don't give up. Down times can be turned to great times. God prospered Abraham irrespective of the prevailing famine in the land. Has God promised to do certain things for you and all that you are experiencing now is difficulty? Hold unto God like Abraham. He will surely perform his promises. Man promises performance, God performs promises.

'Now the LORD had said unto Abram, Get thee out of thy country, and from thy kindred, and from thy father's house, unto a land that I will show thee: And I will make of thee a great nation, and I will bless thee, and make thy name great; and thou shalt be a blessing: And I will bless them that bless thee, and curse him that curseth thee: and in thee shall all families of the earth be blessed'- Gen. 12:1-3

The call to the journey of greatness began with Abraham. God called and made of him a great nation. Abraham was so relevant in the program of God that he was consulted before the divine inferno that engulfed Sodom and Gomorrah.

'And the LORD said, Shall I hide from Abraham that thing which I do; Seeing that Abraham shall surely become a great and mighty nation, and all the nations of the earth shall be blessed in him? For I know him, that he will command his children and his household after him, and they shall keep the way of the LORD, to do justice and judgment; that the LORD may bring upon Abraham that which he hath spoken of him'- Gen. 18:17-19

God seeks to manifest His greatness in and through us. He identified with Abraham and made him great. Are you available for God to display His greatness? There are three principal things to know about Abraham that made him really great:

1. **Obedience:** Abraham yielded implicit, prompt and filial obedience when God demanded him to get out of his country to a place He would reveal to him. It was moving away from a known to an unknown region. *'So Abram departed, as the LORD had spoken unto him; and Lot went with him: and Abram was seventy and five years old when he departed out of Haran'*- Gen. 12:3. In the ladder of greatness, obedience is a step you must

climb to get to the next level. How obedient are you to the word, will and way of God?

2. **Sacrifice:** Abraham waited for 25 years to receive the blessing of God; Isaac. The birth of Isaac brought laughter to the family. It cancelled all the years of shame, ridicule and dryness. And it marked the beginning of the fulfilment of God's promise to Abraham. Family, relatives, friends and well-wishers rejoiced at the coming of the child of promise. Now, Abram could be called Abraham.

'Take now thy son, thine only son Isaac, whom thou lovest, and get thee into the land of Moriah; and offer him there for a burnt offering upon one of the mountains which I will tell thee of. And Abraham rose up early in the morning, and saddled his ass, and took two of his young men with him, and Isaac his son, and clave the wood for the burnt offering, and rose up, and went unto the place of which God had told him'- Gen. 22:2-3

A few years later, God showed up to demand for only one thing from Abraham, his only son. God knocked at Abraham's wooden door to demand for his laughter that lingered in arriving for 25 years. He asked for his Isaac, the child of promise. We can only preach and write about this event as much as we can. Only Abraham who experienced it can tell the story as it is. Experience is certainly the best teacher.

Abraham did not hold back his laughter from God. He willingly, obediently and sacrificially offered his only son to the 'Greater than the greatest'. He surrendered his best to God who makes man to be great. Let me show you the consequence of his action:

'And said, By myself have I sworn, saith the LORD, for because thou hast done this thing, and hast not withheld thy son, thine only son: That in blessing I will bless thee, and in multiplying I will

multiply thy seed as the stars of the heaven, and as the sand which is upon the sea shore; and thy seed shall possess the gate of his enemies; And in thy seed shall all the nations of the earth be blessed; because thou hast obeyed my voice'- Gen. 22:16-18

When God demands our best, it is because He wants to make us great. God promised to make Abraham great. The journey to greatness demands some sacrifice. Abraham did hesitate to give his only son. How sacrificial are you? Is there anything you cannot give to God? Are you willing to give God your 'all', your 'best' when He demands?

3. ***Faith:*** The call to the journey of faith began with Abraham. That is why he is referred to as the father of faith. He left his kindred and country by faith and embarked on a journey he had no details of. He waited by faith for 25 years to receive his first child. And by faith, he agreed to offer his Isaac to God.

'And being not weak in faith, he considered not his own body now dead, when he was about an hundred years old, neither yet the deadness of Sarah's womb: He staggered not at the promise of God through unbelief; but was strong in faith, giving glory to God'- Rom. 4:19-20

'By faith Abraham, when he was called to go out into a place which he should after receive for an inheritance, obeyed; and he went out, not knowing whither he went. By faith he sojourned in the land of promise, as in a strange country, dwelling in tabernacles with Isaac and Jacob, the heirs with him of the same promise: For he looked for a city which hath foundations, whose builder and maker is God'- Heb. 11:8-10

Michael Jordan is a great man

'Don't limit yourself. Many people limit themselves to what they think they can do. You can go as far as your mind lets you. What you believe, remember, you can achieve'- ***Mary Kay Ash***

'Greatness is not measured by what a man or woman accomplishes, but by the opposition he or she has overcome to reach his goals'– *Dorothy Height*

'Whatever the mind of man can conceive and believe, it can achieve'– *Napoleon Hill*

It is said that Mike Jordan's greatest gift isn't his physical ability. His greatest gift is mental discipline. In his career, especially before he blazed forth into meteoric prominence, he was determined from the start, to fully maximize his natural, intrinsic and innate ability.

One of Jordan's closest friends, Ahmad Rashad said: 'Anyone can be like Mike....whatever your field, you can do it'. This is absolutely correct. Anyone can be great. Greatness is not the prerogative of a few, it is rather for the few who choose to be great.

Ahmad Rashad further said, 'Jordan is a normal guy. He just works harder than anyone else'. It was said that Jordan's practice habits amount to an almost alarming harshness. A former Chicago Bulls teammate, B.J Armstrong said about Jordan: 'Michael Jordan is discipline. Not some of the time. Not most of the time. All of the time.

Records are there to show that Jordan was more than a scorer. He was a leader and motivator who took his Bulls to several NBA titles. He usually calls 'practice' more important than the game. His teammates confirmed that he came early to practice and then was the last to leave the pitch. He was an ultimate competitor, quintessential example, punctual and prepared for every tournament.

There are several areas of life that you must institute discipline if you will succeed in maximizing your potentials. Greatness demands great discipline. This great NBA star always exercised discipline. Look at his remark: 'You must expect great things of yourself before you can do them'- *Michael Jordan*

Abraham Lincoln was a great man

"Greatness is not found in possessions, power, position, or prestige. It is discovered in goodness, humility, service and character"- William Arthur Ward

"No one has ever achieved greatness without dreams"- Roy Bennett

"You must remain focused on your journey to greatness"- Les Brown

"There has never been any great person who never met great trials and oppositions but their patience, tenacity, endurance and perseverance saw them to the end as great people" – Ernest Agyemang Yeboah

Abraham Lincoln's rise from humble beginnings to achieving the highest office in the land is a remarkable story. This awkward-gawky lawyer turned politician did not brook any resistance in his ventures and journey to greatness because he knew the inherent seed of greatness in him. In 1860, he was elected as American's 16th president. He was regarded as one of America's greatest heroes due to his role as savior of the Union and emancipator of the slaves.

Abraham Lincoln was not just a legal icon, he was an astute politician. His definite purpose, unflinching determination and bull dog persistence aided him in his journey to greatness. He was persistent and consistent. To him, failure is not final. That you failed does not make you a failure. You can succeed where you failed before. He was an example of his perspective.

In 1832: He lost his job. He was also defeated for state legislature
1n 1833: He failed in business
In 1835: He lost his wife
In 1836: He had nervous breakdown
In 1838: He was defeated for Speaker

In 1843: He was defeated for nomination for Congress
In 1848: He lost nomination again
In 1849: He was rejected for land officer
In 1854: He was defeated for U.S. Senate
In 1856: He was defeated for nomination for Vice President
In 1858: Again, he was defeated for U.S. Senate
In 1860: He was elected President of the United States of America.

Several leaders and successful people have been inspired to heights of greatness by Abraham Lincoln's pedestal of success. He never gave up his dreams because he failed. He persistently continued in his drive until he was elected president of America. Some of his famous quotes include:

'You can fool all the people some of the time, and some of the people all the time, but you cannot fool all the people all of the time'- **Abraham Lincoln**

'Character is like a tree and reputation like its shadow. The shadow is what we think of it; the tree is the real thing'- **Abraham Lincoln**

'I have always found that mercy bears richer fruits than strict justice'- **Abraham Lincoln**

'And in the end, it is not the years in your life that count, it's the life in your years'- **Abraham Lincoln**

'Always bear in mind that your own resolution to succeed is more important than any one thing'- **Abraham Lincoln**

'The best way to predict your future is to create it'- **Abraham Lincoln**

'Give me six hours to chop down a tree and I will spend the first four sharpening the axe' – **Abraham Lincoln**

'I am not concerned that you have fallen, I am concerned that you arise'– **Abraham Lincoln**

David was a great man

David was great in all ramifications. He was a great song writer, musician, king and prophet. He was a man after God's heart who fulfilled the will of God. This great man ousted the Jebusites from the mount, brought back the Ark of the Lord from Philistine, renamed the mountain territory he conquered as Mount Zion, the City of David and instituted a new order of worship. Let us examine the virtues of this great man

DILIGENT: David was diligent in the field as a shepherd boy. At times when young boys idle away in odd places, he was always tendering the flock. His greatness started with his due diligence as a little shepherd boy. Several years later, He exhibited diligence as king over the sheep of God's pasture.

'Seest thou a man diligent in his business? he shall stand before kings; he shall not stand before mean men'-Proverbs 22:29.

Woe unto those who are at ease in Zion. Dearly beloved, you must not be slothful in business. In ministry, work place or business, it behooves the believer to employ persistent and diligent efforts in discharge of assignments. Whatever your hand finds to do, do it with all your might.

David was diligent. In the construction of the tabernacle, he exhibited extreme diligence. In the eviction of the Jebusites, he did it diligently.

Woe unto them that are at ease in Zion. David was not at ease until the Ark rested on the Holy hill. From the account of the historic retrieval of the Ark from the house of Abinada in Kirjathjearim, David was on his toes, painstakingly and assiduously providing the necessary guide and encouragement Israel needed.

ACCOUNTABLE

'And David said unto Saul, Thy servant kept his father's sheep, and there came a lion, and a bear, and took a lamb out of the flock: And I went out after him, and smote him, and delivered it out of his mouth: and when he arose against me, I caught him by his beard, and smote him, and slew him'- 1Samuel 17:34-35

David was accountable. He tended the flock with a high sense of accountability. When a predator wanted to pick a sheep in the flock, he rose up in fury to deliver the prey. That which was committed to him was preserved in his custody. He did not tend the flock with careless abandon.

God will require you to give account of your stewardship (Lk.16:2). Jesus, the noble man in Luke 19 has since gone to obtain his kingdom. He left us here to occupy till he comes. We are in charge. In whatever capacity you minister or work in the spiritual or circular world, God demands that you be accountable because you will render account of your life and ministry.

David was accountable and responsible. When he was to visit the camp of Israel to see how his brothers fared, he left the flock in the custody of another accountable and responsible fellow. He did not abandon the animals. He was responsible enough to delegate authority.

*'And David rose up early in the morning, and left the sheep with a keeper, and took, and went, as Jesse had commanded him; and he came to the trench, as the host was going forth to the fight, and shouted for the battle'-*1 Samuel 17:20

A SINCERE WORSHIPPER

*'And David and all Israel played before God with all their might, and with singing, and with harps, and with psalteries, and with timbrels, and with cymbals, and with trumpets'-*1 Chronicle 13:8.

His life was entirely wrapped up in sincere worship of God. There are prayer warriors. David was a praise warrior. He ministered with his instrument of music in the house of Saul. During the return of the Ark to Zion, David manifested publicly his private worship attitude until the robe that he wound around him dropped off him. And when Micah, his wife despised him for praising God until he was uncovered, he said: *'It was before the LORD, which chose me before thy father, and before all his house, to appoint me ruler over the people of the LORD, over Israel: therefore will I play before the LORD'*-2 Samuel 6:21.

OPEN TO CHANGE.

David was not only faithful and available, he was teachable. Faced with a crisis of old order, he worked assiduously to pioneer transition to a new order. When he discovered he was taking the Ark to the wrong place, he was open to change.

Are you open to change? If you desire to be great in life, you must be teachable. Jesus chided the religious gladiators of his time for their bigotry. Are you a bigot? A bigot holds on to his opinion in defiance of reasoning. How do you handle rebuke? Is there any one that speaks into your life with enough authority to which if and when they speak, you take heed?

LOVE

David loved Saul, though the latter hated him with passion. When he had an opportunity to kill Saul, love constrained him. That love mingled with tears when news reached him that the man that he loved and cherished (Saul) was dead. Again when the seed of Saul, Ishbosheth was murdered so he could ascend the throne as king over all Israel (for he reigned over Judah at that time), he did not rejoice. Love does not rejoice over evil.

David faced a stronger conspiracy by Absalom, his son. It was so turbulent that he vacated his throne for fear of a possible overthrow. God in his wisdom turned the counsel of Ahitophel into foolishness by the counter counsel of Hushai. Absalom died in the rebellion. David's reaction was amazing:

'And the king was much moved, and went up to the chamber over the gate, and wept: and as he went, thus he said, O my son Absalom, my son, my son Absalom! Would God I had died for thee, O Absalom, my son, my son!-2 Samuel 18:33.

For God so loved the world that He gave His only begotten son. Love gives. David was ready to give his life for Absalom. Love characterized life and ministry. He loved both friends and foes; princes and peasants; high and low. It is not convenient for kings to weep in public places. David disregarded this convention. He wept profusely when Cushi broke the news of Absalom's death. Nothing could restrain him.

PENITENT

People play the blame game or cover up when confronted with their sin. David was penitent. He smote his chest in repentance when Nathan the prophet confronted him with his iniquity. Look at his prayer:

'I acknowledged my sin unto thee, and mine iniquity have I not hid. I said, I will confess my transgressions unto the LORD; and thou forgavest the iniquity of my sin'-Psalms 32:5.

Psalms 51 reveals the broken and contrite heart of this man. He did not cover up. He knew too well the futility of covering up. This is a very rare attitude in the society we live today. People do not take responsibility for their actions.

'He that covereth his sins shall not prosper: but whoso confesseth and forsaketh them shall have mercy'-Proverbs 28:13.

Our relationship with God, spouse and one another must be transparent. How often do we cover up in order to preserve our personality! How terribly do we feign that all is well! We quite easily flaunt the angel in us while we conceal the devil that seethes within!

PATIENCE

When Ishbosheth, Saul's son reigned over the tribes of Israel, David reigned in Hebron over Judah. The entire kingdom was legitimately David's by divine edict. Samuel in Bethlehem first anointed him. That anointing was meant to ultimately place him on the throne after Saul.

Here he was in Hebron over Judah. He was not going to plot the fall of Ishbosheth. He was not going to follow the wrong path to the right throne. For another seven years, he patiently waited to possess his possession. The Bible says he that believeth maketh no haste.

The scripture enjoins us to be patient (James 5:7,8). We must be patient with people and in the pursuit of our vision. We must patiently walk up the ladder of greatness. The Psalmist confirmed it:

'I waited patiently for the LORD; and he inclined unto me, and heard my cry. He brought me up also out of an horrible pit, out of the miry clay, and set my feet upon a rock, and established my goings. And he hath put a new song in my mouth, even praise unto our God: many shall see it, and fear, and shall trust in the LORD'-Ps 40.1

ZEAL AND CONFIDENCE

'And David spake to the men that stood by him, saying, What shall be done to the man that killeth this Philistine....that...defy the armies of the living God'-1Samuel 17:26.

David had a deep concern for the honour and reputation of the Lord God of Israel. He recognized that Goliath was defying the armies of Israel. This sparked enough fire in him to let some steam. At a time when the rank and files were cringing for fear as Goliath growled threateningly at the armies of Israel, David chose to challenge the audacity of the uncircumcised Philistine. He was not going to hang out there and hear the vituperate outpouring of Goliath of Gath. Rather than run away, David ran towards the Philistine to snuff life out of him.

How enthusiastic are you concerning the things of the kingdom? Do you have that irrepressible drive and passion in the discharge of your responsibilities? Is there a deep thirst and hunger in you for the Lord? Are you zealous? Are you passionate?

UNDERSTANDING

Like the men of Issachar who had understanding of times and seasons, David understood his covenant relationship with God. He knew that God had a covenant with his fathers and him by extension. And he knew that Goliath was a gentile, a stranger to the commonwealth of Israel, an ignoble and uncircumcised fellow.

'And David spake to the men that stood by him, saying.....who is this uncircumcised Philistine, that he should defy the armies of the living God?'- 1 Samuel 17:26.

David understood that it was the living God of Israel that delivered him from the lion and bear. He did not arrogate power and wisdom of victory to himself. He did not see himself as a whiz kid like some people do today.

*'David said moreover, The LORD that delivered me out of the paw of the lion, and out of the paw of the bear, he will deliver me out of the hand of this Philistine'-*1 Samuel 17:37

His understanding was quick and accurate. He knew it was not a physical but spiritual battle. He understood Goliath was a principality who should be dealt with the amour of God.

Then said David to the Philistine, Thou comest to me with a sword, and with a spear, and with a shield: but I come to thee in the name of the LORD of hosts, the God of the armies of Israel, whom thou hast defied'-1 Samuel 17:43,45.

How apt are we to discern between the workings of the Spirit and the works of the flesh? It is my prayer that the church will have understanding of the ways of God! It is my prayer that *'That the God of our Lord Jesus Christ, the Father of glory, may give unto you the spirit of wisdom and revelation in the knowledge of him: The eyes of your understanding being enlightened; that ye may know what is the hope of his calling, and what the riches of the glory of his inheritance in the saints, And what is the exceeding greatness of his power to us-ward who believe, according to the working of his mighty power.'*-Ephesians 1:17-19

CHAPTER
FOUR

➤

AN ATTITUDE OF CELEBRATION

The mark greatness is celebration. Great people always jubilate. They are cheerful, joyous and excited. You can find them in happy or merry mood any time. Sadness is characteristic of losers. There are several people in this group I call Sad-u see (Sadducees). They see only the sad aspect of life. They are never cheerful or excited.

'And Hannah prayed, and said, My heart rejoiceth in the LORD, mine horn is exalted in the LORD: my mouth is enlarged over mine enemies; because I rejoice in thy salvation'- 1 Sam. 2:1

An attitude of celebration will keep you in the altitude of greatness. Hannah experienced much delay in child bearing and mockery from Peninnah, her rival. She went through a harrowing cycle of pain. Always in sad mood, her many nights of tears aggravated her predicament.

'Then said Elkanah her husband to her, Hannah, why weepest thou? and why eatest thou not? and why is thy heart grieved? am not I better to thee than ten sons?'- 1 Sam. 1:8

This was her prevailing mood for a very long time. She wept profusely in Shiloh because Peninnah provoked her. Neither her tears nor sad countenance could change her condition. Tears don't change ugly situations. They merely vent emotions. She had cried day and night this way for several years without solution. This day, after weeping profusely, Hannah changed her garment of sorrow and put on the attitude of celebration. Greatness was in the offing. She was beginning to realize that joy supersedes sadness. The Fruit of the Spirit includes joy. Hannah found joy in the Lord, the joy that oozes from greatness.

'And she said, Let thine handmaid find grace in thy sight. So the woman went her way, and did eat, and her countenance was no more sad'- 1 Sam. 1:18

Hannah discovered one of the secrets of greatness eventually. She had fallen for Peninnah's mockery and jesting in the past. She had been taunted by friends and neighbours for her infertility. The devil had made her a mincemeat by making her feel insecure and inferior because of her barrenness.

'Her countenance was no more sad'. She had gained mastery over her predicament. She had discovered that weeping may endure for the night but joy comes in the morning. She had realized that 'a merry heart maketh a cheerful countenance: but by sorrow of the heart the spirit is broken' (Prov. 15:13). Her attitude and carriage now depicted greatness.

'And they rose up in the morning early, and worshipped before the LORD, and returned, and came to their house to Ramah: and Elkanah knew Hannah his wife; and the LORD remembered her'- 1 Sam. 1:19

The Lord opened her womb and she gave birth to a notable child. Samuel was a great prophet whose word did not fall to the ground from Dan to Beersheba. From this humble womb came a mighty prophet with a sharp and accurate prophetic precision. Her turning point started from the time she put off the garment of sorrow and put on the attitude of celebration. Like begets like. Your attitude determines your altitude.

WHAT DOES IT MEAN TO CELEBRATE?

To celebrate means to leap for joy. The joy of the Lord is our strength. And the strength of the Lord is our joy. I have written a book titled: OVERFLOWING JOY. You will have a lot to glean from the volume.

'And it came to pass, that, when Elisabeth heard the salutation of Mary, the babe leaped in her womb; and Elisabeth was filled with the Holy Ghost: And she spake out with a loud voice, and said, Blessed art thou among women, and blessed is the fruit of thy womb. And whence is this to me that the mother of my Lord should come to me? For, lo, as soon as the voice of thy salutation sounded in mine ears, the babe leaped in my womb for joy'- Luke 1:41-44

In the Acts of the Apostles, Peter and John were instrumental in stirring up the greatness in the lame man that daily sat at the gate of the temple as a beggar. He got something better than handouts from generous worshippers. He got a miracle! Look at his reaction:

'And he leaping up stood, and walked, and entered with them into the temple, walking, and leaping, and praising God'- Acts 3:8

To celebrate means to rejoice. The Bible says to rejoice always. The joy of the Lord takes away sorrows. It brings everlasting peace within. When David killed Goliath of Gath, there was an eruption of joy. Look at how the people reacted:

'And it came to pass as they came, when David was returned from the slaughter of the Philistine, that the women came out of all cities of Israel, singing and dancing, to meet king Saul, with tabrets, with joy, and with instruments of music'- 1 Sam. 18:6

It is the desire of God that we celebrate always. Rejoicing is one of the ways to celebrate. I have told you earlier that is a mark of greatness. It was a pleasant thing to the inhabitants of the land when David was fetched from Hebron to be enthroned over Israel. It was a day of joy: *'for there was joy in Israel'*

Jerusalem greatly rejoiced when Nehemiah succeeded in building the fallen walls of Jerusalem. Though an uphill task, he got the job done. This triggered joy in the land:

'Also that day they offered great sacrifices, and rejoiced: for God had made them rejoice with great joy: the wives also and the children rejoiced: so that the joy of Jerusalem was heard even afar off'- Neh. 12:43

To celebrate means to testify. Hannah said: My heart rejoiceth in the LORD, mine horn is exalted in the LORD: my mouth is enlarged over mine enemies; because I rejoice in thy salvation.

To celebrate means to laugh. Sarah said: God hath made me to laugh, so that all that hear will laugh with me. Laughter is characteristic of great people. Don't lose sleep over any issue of life. Laugh out in the Lord. The Lord laughs too!

'He that sitteth in the heavens shall laugh: the Lord shall have them in derision'- Psalms 2:4

To celebrate means to experience new beginnings. Your greatness begins when you know that it is your heritage and that you are born to be great. It begins when you wake up to the reality of the inherent greatness in you. It begins when you have an attitude of celebration.

'Remember ye not the former things, neither consider the things of old. Behold, I will do a new thing; now it shall spring forth; shall ye not know it? I will even make a way in the wilderness, and rivers in the desert'- Isa. 43:18-19

AT THE THRESHOLD OF GREATNESS

The journey to greatness is laced with the plans and purposes of God. Halleluiah! The plans of God are good and not evil. He plans to give us great hope and future. Again, the pathway to greatness is iced with the blessings of God. Only those who genuinely thread this path will experience the good things of God. Thus, on your journey to greatness, you will celebrate the following:

Victory: You will find victory on the pathway of greatness. This is what God requires us to celebrate. Joshua was saddled with the responsibility of leading the children of Israel to victory after victory on their journey to greatness; the Promised Land. The Bible gives us detail account of repeated victories under the leadership of this great man. You will encounter greatness as you celebrate victory.

Freedom: You will experience total freedom on the pathway of greatness. Great people are free from what troubles other people. It is time for you to celebrate your freedom in Christ Jesus! You have freedom from sin, sickness, poverty, untimely death, defeat in the hands of the enemy and freedom from fear. Go ahead and celebrate your freedom!

Good News: In our depraved world today, bad news makes good headlines. They are always breaking news. There is nothing bad about the doings of God. God is good all the time. You can only and always have good news in the courts of God. so, celebrate good news. That is your heritage. No evil shall befall you and no plague shall come near your dwelling. Be a carrier of good news. Be a bearer of good things. Spread the goodness of God.

Breakthrough: If you do not embark on a journey, you cannot arrive at the desired destination. Departure certainly determines arrival. There will be breakthrough but you must embark on the journey to greatness. There is no success without venture. The Lord will turn your captivity and you will be like a person who is dreaming but you must begin at once on the journey to greatness. He will fill your mouth with laughter and your tongue with singing. Great things await you on the journey. Begin to celebrate breakthrough in advance.

Fruitfulness: Hannah celebrated her fruitfulness before it became a reality. Greatness is associated with fruitfulness. You will be fruitful. You will have the fruit of the Spirit, the fruit of good works, the fruit of the womb, the fruit of souls of men and the fruit of progress in your endeavours.

Prosperity: great people are always prosperous. And you know it, is our heritage. We are created to show forth the praises and prosperity of God. God prospers His people. It is His will for His children to prosper in all ramifications. As you climb up the ladder of greatness, you will be attracting prosperity. Just as water gravitates to the ocean, success gravitates to those who have programmed their minds to attract it. Celebrate your prosperity my friend. It is your turn, it is your time.

WHEN YOU SEASON OF GREATNESS COMES

God will remember you

There is a book of remembrance which only God can open. When He opens this book, you will be remembered where you were once forgotten. You will be accepted where you were once rejected. You will make great progress where you lingered.

'And the God remembered Noah...'- Gen. 8:1

When Noah finished building the Ark, he went in with his family and pair of each animal as commanded by God. The Bible tells us that the Lord shut them in.

'And they that went in went in male and female of all flesh, as God had commanded him: and the LORD shut him in'- Gen. 7:16

It was the LORD that shut the door of the ark. Only God could open the door He shuts. This day, the Lord remembered Noah and opened the door of the ark. Have you been shut in? The Lord will remember you like He remembered Noah. He keeps a book of remembrance.

He remembered Noah, He will remember you.
He remembered Mordecai, He will remember you.
He remembered Joseph in the prison, He will remember you.
He remembered Hezekiah, He will remember you.
He remembered Israel in Egypt, He will remember you.
He remembered Rachael and opened her womb, He will remember you
He remembered Ruth and gave her Obed, He will remember you
He remembered Hannah and gave her Samuel, He will remember you.

After several years of being forgotten, the Federal Government of Nigeria eventually remembered Pa Taiwo Akinkumi who designed the Nigerian national flag and honoured him. Subsequent governments forgot to honour him until the book of remembrance that only God can open was opened.

The Lord will remember you my friend. Your labour of love will not be in vain. Your tithes, offerings, prophetic seeds, project offering and all kinds of offerings you have made will not be in vain. The Lord will remember you in due season. You will get double blessings for all your troubles. You will get out of adversity for prosperity.

Divine protection from the Lord

'But let all those that put their trust in thee rejoice: let them ever shout for joy, because thou defendest them: let them also that love thy name be joyful in thee'- Psalms 5:11

'As the mountains are round about Jerusalem, so the LORD is round about his people from henceforth even for ever'– Psalms 125:2

In my book titled ENFORCING YOUR DOMINION, I talked about the story of an old woman who lived in a small house by the territory of the enemy in the Second World War. Let me relate it here verbatim: The soldiers were going from house to house to destroy the enemies' camp when they saw the small house riddled with bullets. They knocked hard on the door until an old lady of about 60 opened the door.

Old lady: Who is disturbing my peace? I kept vigil with my master and now I should be resting!

Soldier: Are you not afraid?

Old lady: Afraid of what?

Soldier: Don't you know that you are in the battle front?

Old lady: And so?

Soldier: Don't you know you can be killed?

Old lady: He that keeps me will neither sleep nor slumber. Have you finished with me, I want to go and sleep.

Dearly beloved, you must learn to cast your burdens on the Lord. Rest in Him. Rely totally on the Holy Spirit. Your daily victory is guaranteed. God is committed to those who are committed to Him. Let me give you the Biblical example of the Ravens that God sent to feed Elijah day and night for forty days:

'Get thee hence, and turn thee eastward, and hide thyself by the brook Cherith that is before Jordan. And it shall be, that thou shalt drink of the brook; and I have commanded the ravens to feed thee there. So he went and did according

unto the word of the LORD: for he went and dwelt by the brook Cherith that is before Jordan. And the ravens brought him bread and flesh in the morning, and bread and flesh in the evening; and he drank of the brook'- 1 Kings 17:3-6

The ravens were on mission for God. They were on divine assignment to bring food to Elijah in the morning and evening for forty days. While the assignment lasted, the ravens were safe. They were covered under the shadow of the Almighty God. They were secured from hunters. No hunter could have been able to shoot them down because of this Divine covering.

This is how safe you are under the shadow of His greatness. You will have divine protection from the enemy of righteousness. No evil shall befall you and no plague shall come nigh your dwelling. As the enemies come in one way, they shall flee in seven ways. No weapon that is fashioned against you will prosper. The Lord will disappoint the devices of the crafty so that they will not be able to perform their enterprise.

Miracles and blessings will not pass over you

Jacob was a great man. The blessing the Angel of the Lord carried could not pass over him at Jabbok. He had earnestly prayed: 'I will not let thee go, except thou bless me'. He received the blessing of the Lord.

'And he said, Thy name shall be called no more Jacob, but Israel: for as a prince hast thou power with God and with men, and hast prevailed'- Gen. 32:28

There is this pathetic story of an impotent man who hung around the pool Bethesda for thirty eight years. Miracles passed him by every year. While other sick folks received their healings and miracles after the annual stirring of the waters, he was always left in his pathetic condition. It took the intervention of the Greater than the greatest to get him out of his predicament. Jesus is the Greater than the greatest. He is our greatness.

You may have missed several opportunities in life. Don't give up, it is your turn to experience the miracles and blessings of God. This is your moment of restoration. What you have been looking for will look for and find you. You are at the threshold of greatness.

Your mourning will be turned to dancing

'Thou hast turned for me my mourning into dancing: thou hast put off my sackcloth, and girded me with gladness'- Psalms 30:11

'When the LORD turned again the captivity of Zion, we were like them that dream. Then was our mouth filled with laughter, and our tongue with singing: then said they among the heathen, The LORD hath done great things for them. The LORD hath done great things for us; whereof we are glad'- Psalms 126:1-3

Merriment, singing, dancing and laughing are characteristic of greatness. Your mourning will be turned into dancing. You have no business with sorrow. It is the joy of the Lord to see you happy. May your life, family, ministry and business be wrapped up in the atmosphere of joy in Jesus name.

'Thou shalt increase my greatness, and comfort me on every side'- Psalms 71:21

Your tears will be wiped away

'And God shall wipe away all tears from their eyes; and there shall be no more death, neither sorrow, nor crying, neither shall there be any more pain: for the former things are passed away'- Rev. 21:4

God is a Specialist in wiping away tears from the eyes of people. It is the devil and his wicked forces that make people cry. Jesus went about doing good and healing all that were oppressed by the devil. He is still in the business of wiping away tears. He wiped away the tears of the widow of Nain whose only son died. Her tears gave way laughter afterwards.

'Now when he came nigh to the gate of the city, behold, there was a dead man carried out, the only son of his mother, and she was a widow: and much people of the city was with her. And when the Lord saw her, he had compassion on her, and said unto her, Weep not. And he came and touched the bier: and they that bare him stood still. And he said, Young man, I say unto thee, Arise. And he that was dead sat up, and began to speak. And he delivered him to his mother'- Luke 7:12-15

CHAPTER
FIVE

➡️

SPIRITUAL STEPS TO GREATNESS

There are certain steps you must take in order to climb up the ladder of greatness in whatever endeavour in life. Greatness is a prize. There is a price to pay to get the prize. The steps to greatness are like a coin that has two sides. The sides are spiritual and ethical. In this chapter, I shall discuss some spiritual steps and in the next chapter, ethical steps to greatness.

Join the winning side

Jesus is the commander of the winning side. He is the source of greatness. If you want to be great, join the army of the Great Commander. I have said it for the umpteenth time that the way God relates with the believer is different from the way He relates with the unbeliever. An unbeliever can do certain things at get away with it. His conscience will not prick him. He does not have the Holy Spirit to contend with. He does not have to pray in order to be mischievous, dubious or diabolic.

'Jesus answered and said unto him, Verily, verily, I say unto thee, Except a man be born again, he cannot see the kingdom of God'- John 3:3

For the believer in Christ, the first prerequisite to greatness is being born again. As a believer, you are a member of His body and model of His character. You are His reflection. You are saved to project His image, show forth the praises of He that called you and become His ambassador on earth.

If you want to be great, you must identify with the giver of greatness. Your life must glorify the God of greatness. You must quite the life of sin. SIN is Success In Nothing. Your life must please God. you must shun evil practices, short cuts and abracadabra.

'And he saith unto them, Follow me, and I will make you fishers of men'- Matt. 4:19

Upon leaving Nazareth, Jesus came to Capernaum which was near the sea coast. One day, as He walked by the sea of Galilee, He saw two brothers, Peter and Andrew and called them to follow Him. He said: *'Follow me and I will make you…'* Jesus is a maker. He makes people great. He makes the poor rich, the beggar to become a giver and the servant to become a master. He makes blind people to see, the lame to walk and the deaf to hear. There is only one condition: *'Follow me and I will make you'*.

Do you want to be great in life? Follow Jesus who makes little people great. Give up your sinful lifestyle, surrender to the Commander of greatness and let your life be completely yielded to His word. If you take this first step, you would be on the journey to greatness, *ceteris paribus*.

Have faith in God

Faith plays an indispensable role in the journey of greatness. God honours faith and faith honours God. Without faith, it is impossible to please God. The greater than the greatest that will make you great preeminently demands your faith.

'And Jesus answering saith unto them, Have faith in God….. Therefore I say unto you, What things soever ye desire, when ye pray, believe that ye receive them, and ye shall have them'- Mark 11:22, 24

Do you desire greatness in life? The onus is with you to have faith in God. Pray and believe that God will make you great. Trust God with all your heart. Hold on to His word and demonstrate your faith by having no carnal options. You will be great in life if you do what His word prescribes.

Believe and declare the word of God

Believe and say what God says. God says you are blessed. Believe it, say it. God says you are more than conqueror through Christ. Let this be your confession. What you believe and say has a significant impact in your life. If you say you cannot, you will not. If you say you are finished, you will be finished.

When Moses sent twelve men to spy the land of Canaan, they came back with different reports. Ten of them brought negative report. According to them, they were like grasshoppers in the sight of the giants that occupied the land. Joshua and Caleb brought back a positive report. They declared they could conquer the giants and take over the land that flowed with milk and honey.

Now, the children of Israel believed the evil report of the ten spies. They believed and declared that they were little, weak, powerless and unable to overcome the giants and possess the land. They believed and declared that they were like grasshoppers in the sight of the inhabitants of the land. Look at the verdict of God:

'Say unto them, As truly as I live, saith the LORD, as ye have spoken in mine ears, so will I do to you: Your carcases shall fall in this wilderness; and

all that were numbered of you, according to your whole number, from twenty years old and upward, which have murmured against me, Doubtless ye shall not come into the land, concerning which I sware to make you dwell therein, save Caleb the son of Jephunneh, and Joshua the son of Nun'- Numbers 13:28-30

What you believe and declare will come to pass eventually. All adults from twenty years and above perished in the wilderness according to their confession. They confessed they could not possess the land because of the stronger occupants of the land. They confessed they would be defeated and destroyed. That is what they got!

Whose report will you believe? You have a choice to believe that you have a terminal disease or that Jesus took away your infirmities and bore your diseases. You have a choice to believe that you are weak or that you are strong in the Lord and in the power of His might. You have a choice to believe and declare that you are little or that you are great because greater is He that is in you than he that is in the world. Brethren, you have a choice to believe that the enemy is stronger or that you are stronger than your enemy! The choice is exclusively yours! If you believe, make the following declarations in Jesus name:

I have dominion.
I have dominion over sin.
I have dominion over satan.
I have dominion over sickness.
I have dominion over diseases.
I have dominion over fear.
I have dominion over self.
I have dominion over situations.
I have dominion over failure.

My defense is impenetrable. I am safe and secure in Christ Jesus. No evil shall befall me and no plague shall come nigh my dwelling. I am a winner and not a loser. I am the head and not the tail. I am above and not beneath. I am victorious because He is a Victor. I am a conqueror because He conquered. Yeah, I am more than a conqueror through Christ!

My destiny shall not be truncated. My glory shall not be subdued. My place shall no man take. I am making meaningful progress in all my endeavors. I have no limitations.

I cannot be stopped by evil forces. I cannot be frustrated from the pathway of greatness. I am not a weakling. I am strong in the Lord and in the power of his might; stronger than my enemies; stronger than principalities and powers. I am an overcomer for greater is He that is in me than he that is in the world. I am from above, siting with Christ in the heavenly places. The world is under my feet for in Christ Jesus is the victory that overcomes the world.

In Jesus name, I exercise absolute dominion over all oppositions and unpleasant circumstances of life. I rule my world in dominion. I rule and reign as king on earth in Jesus name. The world is under my feet. Satan, sin and sickness are under my feet. I trample over principality and powers. I have lordship over the forces of darkness in Jesus name. I sit with Christ in the heavenly places in dominion.

I am unbeatable, unreachable and irrepressible. I walk tall, shoulder high and head up. I cannot be intimidated. I take cue from the Lion of the tribe of Judah. Like the lion, I am bold, strong and fearless. There is no mountain too high for me to conquer. There is no wall too impregnable for me. And there is no troop too formidable for me. I am a champion, a winner and a victor in Jesus name. AMEN!

Have sound knowledge

'And such as do wickedly against the covenant shall he corrupt by flatteries: but the people that do know their God shall be strong, and do exploits'- Dan. 11:32

You must know your rights and privileges in Christ if you must ascend the ladder of greatness. Jesus said in John 8:32 that you shall know the truth and the truth will make you free. It is the truth you know that will make you free. There are principles to life. There are principles for health, prosperity, knowledge, church growth, wisdom, long life and son on. It is your job to search the scriptures and find them.

Sometimes, it is not by fasting and prayer but by knowledge. You must study the word of God to get yourself approved. You must be addicted to and saturated with the word of God. The word of God carries the power of God. I you want to be great in life, be addicted to the word of God. Get the word! Be saturated with the word! Dig deep to grow great!

Develop a dynamic prayer life

Prayer is not a hit and run business like people take it. Some people pray only when they have problems or when they need a blessing from God. This is not what I am talking about. Prayer is not a once in a while affair.

Your life is God's business. You are His workmanship but you must pray to enforce the will of God in your life. Pray, don't be a prey to sin, satan, sickness, self and storms of life. Prayer is steps you up in the ladder of greatness. I have never met a person that is genuinely successful who does not have a dynamic prayer life.

Prayer is an indispensable aspect of the believer's walk with God. Jesus demonstrated a prayer life and taught His disciples to pray. He prayed very early in the morning. He prayed all night too. He prayed always. His life and ministry was characterized by prayer.

'And he spake a parable unto them to this end, that men ought always to pray, and not to faint'- Luke 18:1

Ask the Lord to lead you in the path of greatness. Seek the Lord as you embark on the processes that lead to greatness in life. Take authority over the devil and all forms of unpleasant conditions. Bind and loose. Cast out and command. Speak to the mountains to move yonder. Tell the storm to cease. Command the devils to stop their repulsive activities.

'Verily I say unto you, Whatsoever ye shall bind on earth shall be bound in heaven: and whatsoever ye shall loose on earth shall be loosed in heaven'- Matt. 18:18

Believe in the prophet of God over your life

'And Elijah the Tishbite, who was of the inhabitants of Gilead, said unto Ahab, As the LORD God of Israel liveth, before whom I stand, there shall not be dew nor rain these years, but according to my word'- 1 Kings 17:1

Elijah stood in his office as a prophet and declared that there will be neither rain nor dew for forty two months. God said amen to his declaration. There was neither rain nor dew according to the word of the man of God. Who is your spiritual head? Do you have one?

'Then Elisha said, Hear ye the word of the LORD; Thus saith the LORD, To morrow about this time shall a measure of fine flour be sold for a shekel, and two measures of barley for a shekel, in the gate of Samaria'- 2 Kings 7:1

Elisha, his successor also declared that there will be abundance of food in Samaria within twenty four hours in the midst of an acute famine. God said amen to his declaration. Four lepers simply tip-toed through the Syrian gate and the Lord turned their fragile steps to the noise of chariots, horses and battalions. The inhabitants of the land were stampeded out of their land and the abundance of the county was hurled to Samaria. There was abundance of food according to the word of Elisha.

'And they rose early in the morning, and went forth into the wilderness of Tekoa: and as they went forth, Jehoshaphat stood and said, Hear me, O Judah, and

ye inhabitants of Jerusalem; Believe in the LORD your God, so shall ye be established; believe his prophets, so shall ye prosper'– 2 Chron. 20:20

Having instructed Jehoshaphat how to handle and defeat the allied forces of Ammon, Moab and Mount Seir, God told him to tell the children of Israel to 'Believe in the LORD your God, so ye shall be established; believe his prophets, so ye shall PROSPER'.

God is a God of order. He has set leadership in place to cater for His people. Your pastor or whoever is the head of your church or ministry has spiritual oversight of the congregation. As there is hierarchy in physical authority, there is hierarchy in spiritual authority. There are certain battles that hinder prosperity that he can win for you. If you do not believe and honour him, you will not benefit from his spiritual authority. **If you despise your prophet, you will forfeit your prosperity**.

'He that receiveth a prophet in the name of a prophet shall receive a prophet's reward; and he that receiveth a righteous man in the name of a righteous man shall receive a righteous man's reward'– Matt. 10:42

Your pastor or spiritual leader is God's representative. Do you honour him? Do you believe him? Do you bless him financially and materially? Do you pray for him? How you treat him determines how God will treat you. God says you will prosper if you take care of your pastor. The ball is in your court. You can fast and pray for prosperity but taking care of your spiritual leader is a cheaper and quicker option. The choice is exclusively yours!

Honour the Lord with your substance

'Honour the LORD with thy substance, and with the first fruits of all thine increase: So shall thy barns be filled with plenty, and thy presses shall burst out with new wine'– Prov. 3:9-10

'Will a man rob God? Yet ye have robbed me. But ye say, Wherein have we robbed thee? In tithes and offerings. Ye are cursed with a curse: for ye have robbed me, even this whole nation. Bring ye all the tithes into the storehouse, that there may be meat in mine house, and prove me now herewith, saith the LORD of hosts, if I will not open you the windows of heaven, and pour you out a blessing, that there shall not be room enough to receive it. And I will rebuke the devourer for your sakes, and he shall not destroy the fruits of your ground; neither shall your vine cast her fruit before the time in the field, saith the LORD of hosts'- Mal. 3:8-10

First fruit, offerings and tithes are spiritual exercises. There is a correlation between these offerings and overall success in life. Let me make a simple distinction between them:

First fruit is your first earning or profit. When you get a new job, your first earning is your first fruit. When you start a new business, your first profit is your first fruit. When you are promoted from one level to another, the difference between the former and new level is your first fruit. It is the Lord's. For example, if you earn N150, 000 monthly and you are promoted to now earn N195, 000, the first N45, 000 that marks your increase is your first fruit.

Offering is what you willingly give for the furtherance of the gospel of Christ. The Philippian church prospered immensely because they gave offering to further the gospel. If you must great, give. Honour the Lord with your substance.

Tithe is the tenth part or 10% of your salary or profit if you are a businessman or woman. It belongs to God. It is your seed. It depends on you to give it or withhold it. But the bible clearly tells us that it is not yours.

What is the promise for those who honour the Lord with their first fruit? *So shall thy barns be filled with plenty, and thy presses shall burst out with new wine'*- Prov. 3:9-10

Great and successful believers have one thing in common: they give, give and give. They honour the Lord with their substance. They remit their first fruits and pay their tithes. The choice is yours to be willing and obedient to this spiritual principle. But let me make it very clear to you that it is one of the steps you must climb to greatness in life.

CHAPTER
SIX

➡️

ETHICAL STEPS TO GREATNESS

Ethics are principles relating to right or wrong conduct. They are conventional standards that govern specific areas of human life. For example, if you want to excel in sports and entertainment, there specific standards you must follow. This includes discipline, constant training, proper diet, resilience and others.

There are ethical steps to greatness. In chapter five, we placed emphasis on spiritual steps to greatness. In this chapter, let us look at ethical steps to greatness in two broad perspectives:

1. WORK ETHICS
2. MORAL ETHICS

WORK ETHICS

EXCELLENCE:

Great people are always excellent in what they do. This is what distinguishes them from others. Excellence is an indispensable virtue.

There is no one that can achieve great feats of valour without this virtue. You must be excellent in all you do.

Let me make a practical example. The difference between Mr Biggs and other road side restaurants is Excellence. In this case, excellence will include good customer care, cozy environment, ambience, recipe, packaging and delivery. It is a known fact that the caliber of people that patronize Mr Biggs is quite different from those that sit around road side restaurants. And the kind of money Mr Biggs generate is certainly much more than what owners of road side restaurants make.

The difference between these eateries is excellence. The strength of one (Excellence) is the weakness of the other. People pay more for excellence. The taste of the food and quantity of it may be the same but where a person excitedly pays N7, 000 for a full course in Mr Biggs, he may be reluctant to pay N1, 500 elsewhere. Excellence gives the edge.

Just as water gravitates naturally to the ocean, greatness gravitates towards people who are prepared and equipped to attract it. Excellence is one of such equipment. There are people who have a knack for excellent products and services. Rather than transact with the mediocre, they will look out for excellent people who will give them what they want. It does not matter how much more they will pay; all they want is excellent product or service.

'Whatsoever thy hand findeth to do, do it with thy might...'- Eccl. 9:10

As you embark on the journey to greatness, you will do well to employ and apply excellent principles. There is no room for mediocrity in the 21st century. People are looking for impeccable technocrats. Excellent delivery is very essential in any endeavour. Be excellent in what you do. Give it your best. Go the extra mile. Go beyond limits. Greatness is a process even though it is inherent. Its manifestation is a process and an attitude of greatness must be cultivated in order to have a practical experience of greatness.

Strive to make a difference in whatever you do. Be excellent. Do it excellently. With the rate of the available technology, the world in which we live is like a global village. Your excellence could take you somewhere. And well too, your mediocrity will take you nowhere. Let me make it very plain to you that there is no job that is not lucrative. It is only a matter of creativity. Until you are creative, you may not be lucrative.

The drug Clerk, Asa Candler bought an old kettle for five hundred dollar from an old county Doctor. That was the kettle from which coca cola was sold. Fortunes started to flow from the kettle when he added one more ingredient, *imagination.* He bottled the flowing liquid. Today, the bottled content speaks for itself in every nation of the world. Add one more ingredient: *excellence* and you will stand out.

God is excellent. Everything about his kingdom is excellent. He expects you to be excellent too. As a believer, there is a seed of excellence in you. The nature of Christ in you is excellent. With God, there is no second-rater. Excellence is associated with Him. *Excellent is your name oh Lord!* Harness this implicit virtue and apply it in all you do. Aim high! Dream big! Perform beyond expectation. This is what will distinguish you from other people in your area of jurisdiction. Keep the standard or exceed it as much as you can.

'Then this Daniel was preferred above the presidents and princes because an excellent spirit was in him...'- Daniel 6:3

An excellent spirit was in Daniel. Way back the Old Testament! We are in a better covenant. Our Commander-In-Chief has laid for us an example to follow and He enables us to follow in His steps. Everything about Jesus is excellent. Be excellent in all of your endeavours. Demonstrate an excellent spirit and surround yourself with people who seek excellence. Avoid pessimists. Do away with myopic and mental pigmies.

Let excellence be your motto and dictum. Be an embodiment of excellence. Be extraordinary in your presentations. Let your approach be flawless. Exude that aura of excellence that set people in awe. Pull the strings of the extra in ordinary. You will be extraordinary. You will be irresistible. You will be a sought-after.

RIGHT DECISION

Taking right, prompt and smart decisions is very vital in the journey to greatness. Your decision yesterday is the reason you are where you are today. Your decision today will determine where you will be tomorrow. Great people often take great decisions.

Some people are very poor in decision making. They make poor judgments and take wrong steps. Be smart and calculated in decision making. Make correct analysis. One right decision can take you to the top. One wrong decision can plunge you to the bottom. So, look before you leap!

INDUSTRY

'In all labour there is profit: but the talk of the lips tendeth only to penury'- Prov. 14:23

'Seeth thou a man diligent in his business? He shall stand before kings; he shall not stand before mean men'- Proverbs 22:29

'Whatsoever thy hands findeth to do, do it with thy might...'- Eccl. 9:10

God only prospers the works of our hands. He does not prosper mere desires. You must put your hands to work! You cannot be great if you refuse to work. Plan your work and work out your plan. God does not bless laziness. Be diligent. Let this be your watchword.

Abraham was a great man. He wasn't great because here merely wished to be great. He reared cattle.

Isaac was a great man. Irrespective of the fact that he inherited Abraham's success, he worked hard and he dug wells. Greatness did not fall on his laps like a ripe mango from the mango tree.

Jacob was a great man. This great man was the hub of Laban's business. He was so diligent with Laban's flocks in spite of being shortchanged. The God of compensation settled him eventually.

'And he shall be like a tree planted by the rivers of water, that bringeth forth his fruit in his season; his leaf also shall not wither; and whatsoever he doeth shall prosper'- Psalms 1:3

There is no substitute for diligence. Joseph was so diligent that he earned the respect of his master, Potiphar. He was put in charge of the entire Potiphar's holdings. He was a great man in the prison. And he was great in Pharaoh's cabinet.

'Seeth thou a man diligent in his business? He shall stand before kings; he shall not stand before mean men'- Proverbs 22:29

VISION

"Where there is no vision, the people perish'- Proverbs 29:18

Vision is like a compass that gives you direction. You need vision to help you navigate your way in life, ministry or business. You need vision to drive you up the ladder of greatness. Without vision, you may never make meaningful progress and achieve great things in life.

Several people have no vision but television. They spend hours every day watching the television. Greatness is a serious business. It takes vision to be great. Vision places you ahead. It puts you in a vantage position to navigate through the vicissitudes of life. Don't sit before the television all your life! Get a vision and stand vehemently by it! Those you watch on the television have their vision. That's why they are celebrated. That's why you are watching them. You too can be watched in the television. Get a vision if you want to be watched in the television! Let me counsel you ladies; don't follow a man because he has television. Follow a man that has vision. His vision will buy him television eventually.

WISDOM

'If any of you lack wisdom, let him ask of God, that giveth to all men liberally, and upbraideth not; and it shall be given you'- James 1:5

'Get wisdom, get understanding: forget it not neither decline from the words of my mouth. Forsake her not and she shall preserve thee: live her, and she shall keep thee. Wisdom is the principal thing; therefore, get wisdom: and with all thy getting, get understanding'- Proverbs 4:5-7

Successful men and women are preeminently men and women of wisdom. Wisdom is their principal tool. God will empower you with skills, knowledge and abilities but you will need wisdom to properly channel your endowment. Wisdom is a necessary tool for accomplishment of goals and aspirations. Wisdom is vital to greatness in life. It is an indispensable key in the pursuit success in life.

All our patriarchs, some of whom are mentioned in this book were endowed with the wisdom that comes from God. Abraham was not bankrupt of wisdom. Isaac had great wisdom in dealing with oppositions. Jacob applied wisdom to survive in Laban's house of troubles. He got his portion of flocks by wisdom.

How did Joseph get out of incarceration? By wisdom! How did he rise to the top as Prime Minister in a foreign land? By wisdom! He resolved the dreams of the baker and butler. He solved the life threatening problem of a nation. He answered the question of national economic security. The solution he brought before Pharaoh was outstanding.

Wisdom is like a game changer. There is no price too much to pay for this priceless treasure. It is essential in relationships. It is essential in business transactions. Lack of it makes you vulnerable.

Wisdom is an indispensable tool in the pursuit of greatness. It gives you leverage and brings you above board. It makes you take intelligent and fruitful decisions. Wisdom will shed light to life threatening problems and proffer an impeccable panacea. It gives you answer to questions and solutions to critical problems. Wisdom makes you vibrant, resilient and indomitable.

Wisdom will make you fast and pray to seek the face of God. Wisdom will make you dwell in peace with your spouse. Wisdom will make you obey spiritual laws that govern prosperity. Wisdom will enable you to make right choices. Wisdom will put you on track. Friend, you need wisdom in your journey to greatness.

CONSISTENCE AND PERSISTENCE

Be business-like: smart, swift and sharp.
Make use of every opportunity you find.
Maximize your time. Don't waste it.
Be punctual. Punctuality is the soul of business.
Be consistent. A rolling stone gathers no moss.
Be persistent. Don't give up too soon. Don't ever give up.

CAPACITY BUILDING

Acquire new skills and aptitudes. Be abreast of your contemporaries. Gather more knowledge as you climb up the ladder of greatness. Be in a vantage position. Strive always to be above board. Make yourself marketable. Be indispensable in your field. Be the one that holds the ace. Be the one that calls the shots!

Greatness is relative and dynamic. It is a never ending process. There is no zenith. So, you must keep increasing your capacity: mental and spiritual. Never be outdated when it comes to knowledge. Keep updated by learning something new when opportunity comes.

MORAL ETHICS

There are certain moral ethics you must observe in the journey to greatness. I will discuss a few of them briefly. This is by no means exhaustive.

FAITHFULNESS

'A faithful man shall abound with blessings: but he that maketh haste to be rich shall not be innocent'- Prov. 28:20

Faithfulness in little things:
'He that is faithful in that which is least is faithful also in much: and he that is unjust in the least is unjust also in much'- Luke 16:10

Faithfulness in another man's business:
'And if ye have not been faithful in that which is another man's, who shall give you that which is your own?'- Luke 16:12

Faithfulness is money:
'If therefore ye have not been faithful in the unrighteous mammon, who will commit to your trust the true riches?'- Luke 16:11

71

Faithfulness in little things

Faithfulness is central to greatness. It begins with little things. No one will commit great responsibilities to your hands if you cannot handle little things faithfully. You must first be faithful and accountable in little things. The more faithful you are, the more you will be trusted to handle bigger things. Jesus made it clear that he that is faithful in little things will be faithful in much.

Let me make a practical example: people misbehave with money and power. If N500, 000 makes you misbehave such that you abuse everyone around you, you will not get N10, 000, 000. That will make you mad. God does not want His children to end up in psychiatric hospitals.

Your character is an indication you will be able to handle greater things if you are given little things to handle. Some people become proud like a peacock when they attain a level of position. They quite easily become abusive. Such people cannot handle higher positions of authority. They will step on the head of people. Are you faithful? It begins with little things.

Faithfulness in another man's business

Jacob was accountable with Laban's flocks. God blessed him until he became very great in his business.

David was accountable with the sheep of his father, Jesse. No wonder God put him in charge of His sheep (Israel).

If you are not faithful in another man's business, you can never make great progress when you have your own. Irresponsibility is an attitude as faithfulness is. If you are unfaithful with another man's business, that attitude will show up when you have your own business.

Be faithful wherever you are, no matter how insignificant it is. Make sure you are faithful in another man's business. This is expedient if you will go forward and become great in life. Wherever you work, handle things as if they are your own. Do it as if it is yours. When you eventually have your own, you will handle it well and prosper. Have what I call *'owner's mentality'* Jacob eventually had a large flock of animals having pre-eminently been faithful in another man's flocks. David was put in charge of the entire people of Israel having preeminently been faithful with his father's sheep.

Faithfulness in money

Money wields so much power and influence. In some quarters, if you place God and money side by side, people will choose the latter.

'…and money is a defence…'- Eccl. 7:12

'…but money answereth all things'- Eccl. 10:19

> "If therefore ye have not been faithful in the
> unrighteous mammon, who will commit to
> your trust the true riches?'- Luke 16:11

If you are not faithful with money, God will not commit things of eternal value to you.

OBEDIENCE AND SERVICE

Your greatness is contingent on your obedience to spiritual principles, moral and work ethics. If you want to be in authority, you must first be under authority. You must be under order. God will avenge every disobedience when your obedience is complete!

'If they obey and serve him, they shall spend their days in prosperity, and their years in pleasures' Job 36:11

Look at Deuteronomy chapter twenty-eight from verse two:

'And all these blessings shall come on thee, and overtake thee, if thou shalt hearken unto the voice of the LORD thy God'

'Blessed shalt thou be in the city, and blessed shalt thou be in the field'

'Blessed shall be the fruit of thy body, and the fruit of thy ground, and the fruit of thy cattle, the increase of thy kine, and the flocks of thy sheep'

'Blessed shall be thy basket and thy store'

'Blessed shalt thou be when thou comest in, and blessed shalt thou be when thou goest out'

'The LORD shall cause thine enemies that rise up against thee to be smitten before thy face: they shall come out against thee one way, and flee before thee seven ways'

'The LORD shall command the blessing upon thee in thy storehouses, and in all that thou settest thine hand unto; and he shall bless thee in the land which the LORD thy God giveth thee'

'The LORD shall establish thee an holy people unto himself, as he hath sworn unto thee, if thou shalt keep the commandments of the LORD thy God, and walk in his ways'

'And all people of the earth shall see that thou art called by the name of the LORD; and they shall be afraid of thee'

'And the LORD shall make thee plenteous in goods, in the fruit of thy body, and in the fruit of thy cattle, and in the fruit of thy ground, in the land which the LORD sware unto thy fathers to give thee'

'The LORD shall open unto thee his good treasure, the heaven to give the rain unto thy land in his season, and to bless all the work of thine hand: and thou shalt lend unto many nations, and thou shalt not borrow'

'And the LORD shall make thee the head, and not the tail; and thou shalt be above only, and thou shalt not be beneath; if that thou hearken unto the commandments of the LORD thy God, which I command thee this day, to observe and to do them'

Obedience is very important to greatness. So is service. Just like an employer pays wages to his workers, so God will make us great us if we serve Him diligently. And just like parents meet the demands of an obedient child, God is poised to prosper and make us really great if we are obedient to Him.

UPRIGHT LIVING

'For the LORD God is a sun and shield: the LORD will give grace and glory: no good thing will he withhold from them that walk uprightly'- Psalms 84:11

There is a place for upright living in the eternal plan and purpose of God. The bible says He will not withhold any good thing from those who walk uprightly. God who makes people great is upright. He demands uprightness from His children. No sane parent will give his treasures to a wayward, rebellious and extravagant child.

'For thou, LORD, wilt bless the righteous; with favour wilt thou compass him as with a shield'- Psalms 5:12

We have the responsibility to live uprightly, remain in his will, way and word. Our commitment in this regard is essential if we desire to be great in life. He will be committed to lavish his favour on those who walk uprightly.

'The righteous shall flourish like the palm tree: he shall grow like a cedar in Lebanon'- Psalms 92:12

'Those that be planted in the house of the LORD shall flourish in the courts of our God'- Psalms 92:13

While in slavery in Potiphar's house, Joseph prospered. God favoured and blessed him. Do you know why Joseph prospered in this unfavourable condition? He was morally upright. He lived in integrity. Many young men of nowadays will sleep with Mrs Potiphar in order to secure their job and curry more favour from her and Potiphar. Joseph refused to be immoral with his master's wife. This was very pleasing to God. God will acknowledge and elevate you eventually if you remain upright.

This upright living and integrity did not begin with him in slavery. Back home when he was with his siblings, he was always giving his father objective reports. He was upright in his dealings. No wonder Jacob loved him so much and gave him a coat of many colours.

'Blessed is the man that walketh not in the counsel of the ungodly, nor standeth in the way of sinners, nor sitteth in the seat of the scornful... and whatsoever he doeth shall prosper'– Psalms 1:1-3

Dearly beloved, you will do well to stay away from evil. Unrighteousness will negate the plan of God for your life. Sin is a reproach! God is committed to prosper those who will stay away from evil. Such people will be like a tree that is planted by the rivers of water, whose leaves shall not wither. Whatsoever they do shall prosper. Do you want to be great? Be upright! Stay away from the counsel of the wicked. Don't stand in the shoes of the sinner. Don't sit in the seat of the scornful.

The prodigal son had a great opportunity which he misused. He had the chance of multiplying the portion of his inheritance. He was already independent but he wasted his resources in frivolities. Some people will multiply their evil when they climb up the ladder of greatness a little. More money, power or success means more women, more clubbing and shadier deals. Set your heart to live a clean and upright life. You will attract God's blessings.

CHAPTER
SEVEN

——————▶

YOUR GREATNESS IS HERE!

Your greatness is here! Hurray!

I have made it clear from the beginning that greatness is your heritage. When you wake up to this reality, you are on your way to greatness. In the hall of greatness, I made specific examples of great people both Biblical and contemporary. I also told you that an attitude of celebration is essential in the altitude of greatness you seek. It was imperative for me to show you practical steps to greatness. I talked about both spiritual and ethical steps to greatness.

Now, your greatness is here! If you are truly abreast of the content of the preceding chapters, then dust your boots and get ready to climb the ladder of greatness. It is your turn, it is your time to be great. You will experience the following as indications that your greatness is actually here:

Mercy will speak for you

'Thou shalt arise, and have mercy upon Zion: for the time to favour her, yea, the set time, is come'- Psalms 102:13

'So then it is not of him that willeth, nor of him that runneth, but of God that showeth mercy'- Rom. 9:16

You will find the mercy of God. His mercy will prevail over judgment. God will take away calamities from you and shield you from arrows of darkness. You will be like a cat that has nine lives. The Lord will fight your battles for you.

Have you been experiencing the mercy of God? Keep your eyes ever on Him. The sure mercies of David will keep you all the way.The steadfast love of the Lord never ceases. His mercies are new every morning. Great is His faithfulness.

No giant can stop you

Goliath of Gath intimidated the armies of Israel for forty days. He spoke with such audacity and supercilious demeanor that the men of war groveled at his feet. They were too scared to dare him as a veteran of war. He had been a warrior from his youth.

For forty days, nobody from the camp of Israel could pick the challenge. He was unstoppable until David came to the scene. This son of Jesse had no experience of war. His only advantage was the Lord who is mighty in battle. He had saved the flock from the curly paws of a bear and lion. He trusted God that the uncircumcised Philistine would be stopped from harassing the covenant people of God.

'And it came to pass, when the Philistine arose, and came and drew nigh to meet David, that David hasted, and ran toward the army to meet the Philistine'- 1 Sam. 17:48

He was a young lad of ruddy countenance. In fury, Goliath rose up to overrun this youngster and stop his misbehaviour. The Bible tells us that David ran towards him rather than away from him like all other soldiers in the camp did. He was unstoppable by the wicked bear. He was unstoppable by the voracious lion. And now, he would be unstoppable by the uncircumcised philistine.

'And David put his hand in his bag, and took thence a stone, and slang it, and smote the Philistine in his forehead, that the stone sunk into his forehead; and he fell upon his face to the earth. So David prevailed over the Philistine with a sling and with a stone, and smote the Philistine, and slew him; but there was no sword in the hand of David'- 1 Sam. 17:49-50

The young lad was unstoppable. It was an indication that the great God that makes His children great was with him. that is how you will be unstoppable. Your greatness is here!

You will be remembered

'Then spake the chief butler unto Pharaoh, saying, I do remember my faults this day.... Then Pharaoh sent and called Joseph, and they brought him hastily out of the dungeon: and he shaved himself, and changed his raiment, and came in unto Pharaoh'- Gen. 41:9,14

You will be remembered because your greatness is here. When it was time to discharge Joseph from the prison and elevate him to the palace, he was remembered. When it was time for Pa Taiwo Akinkumi, the designer of the Nigerian national flag, to be honoured, the Federal Government of Nigeria remembered him.

'On that night could not the king sleep, and he commanded to bring the book of records of the chronicles; and they were read before the king'- Esther 6:1

'Then they that feared the LORD spake often one to another: and the LORD hearkened, and heard it, and a book of remembrance was written

before him for them that feared the LORD, and that thought upon his name'- Mal. 3:16

When it was time to elevate Mordecai, the book of remembrance was opened. He was honoured instead of being punished according to the evil of Haman. The Lord remembered Hannah and opened her womb as He remembered Rachael.

'And they rose up in the morning early, and worshipped before the LORD, and returned, and came to their house to Ramah: and Elkanah knew Hannah his wife; and the LORD remembered her'- 1 Sam. 1:19

'And God remembered Rachel, and God hearkened to her, and opened her womb'- Gen. 30:22

You will be accepted where you were rejected

Another indication that your greatness is in the offing is that you will be accepted where you were rejected. Those who despised you before will begin to honour you. You will have a yes where you had a no before. You will be celebrated instead of being tolerated.

'And Gilead's wife bare him sons; and his wife's sons grew up, and they thrust out Jephthah, and said unto him, Thou shalt not inherit in our father's house; for thou art the son of a strange woman'- Judges 11:2

Jephthah was rejected by his household members because he was born by 'another woman'. He was denied his rights and privileges in the family of orientation. For a very long time, he was forgotten and abandoned. Nobody reckoned with him.

'And it came to pass in process of time, that the children of Ammon made war against Israel. And it was so, that when the children of Ammon made war against Israel, the elders of Gilead went to fetch Jephthah out of the land of Tob: And they said unto Jephthah, Come, and be our captain, that we may fight with the children of Ammon'- Judges 11:4-6

Several years down the line, the same people that rejected Jephthah went for him. In their time of distress, they remembered the son of a harlot that was thrown out and forgotten. It was time for him to be elevated. They came to invite him to be their captain. You will be remembered my friend. Just keep your focus on God and your dreams intact.

You will be assisted

'So it came to pass, when the king's commandment and his decree was heard, and when many maidens were gathered together unto Shushan the palace, to the custody of Hegai, that Esther was brought also unto the king's house, to the custody of Hegai, keeper of the women. And the maiden pleased him, and she obtained kindness of him; and he speedily gave her her things for purification, with such things as belonged to her, and seven maidens, which were meet to be given her, out of the king's house: and he preferred her and her maids unto the best place of the house of the women'– Esther 2:8-9

Esther was assisted because it was time for her to be honoured and elevated. The king eventually set the royal crown upon her head, and made her queen instead of Vashti. You will be assisted to move up the ladder of greatness. You will be picked out of the queue and assisted. You will find help when you need it.

You will be favoured

'Now when the turn of Esther, the daughter of Abihail the uncle of Mordecai, who had taken her for his daughter, was come to go in unto the king, she required nothing but what Hegai the king's chamberlain, the keeper of the women, appointed. And Esther obtained favour in the sight of all them that looked upon her. So Esther was taken unto king Ahasuerus into his house royal in the tenth month, which is the month Tebeth, in the seventh year of his reign. And the king loved Esther above all the women, and she obtained grace and favour in his sight more than all the virgins; so that he set the royal crown upon her head, and made her queen instead of Vashti'– Esther 2:15-17

Divine favour is an indication that God is at work in your life. Esther found favour because it was her turn to be lifted and crowned. The God that makes His children great is the God that brings favour. He will overwhelm you with favour. You will find favour with God and man.

Favour is receiving what you don't deserve. There certain benefits you will receive that you did not labour for. It is like reaping where you have not sown. When your greatness is here, you will have uncommon favour. You will bask in the glory and favour of God. The Lord will order your steps to great opportunities. You will experience inexplicable favour.

You will receive accelerated promotion

Joseph is a typical example of someone who received accelerated promotion. From the prison, he was brought before king Pharaoh. He never returned to the prison. He experienced very rapid elevation. The king instructed that he be decorated and made to ride on his royal horse.

'And Pharaoh took off his ring from his hand, and put it upon Joseph's hand, and arrayed him in vestures of fine linen, and put a gold chain about his neck; And he made him to ride in the second chariot which he had; and they cried before him, Bow the knee: and he made him ruler over all the land of Egypt'– Gen. 41:42-43

King Pharaoh put his ring in Joseph's finger, and arrayed him in vestures of fine linen and put a gold chain around his neck. Joseph was given a wife and he married almost instantly. There was no room for courtship. He was enthroned and placed in charge of the economy of Egypt. He experienced so much rapid changes that his brothers could not recognize him when they saw him.

There will be divine rearrangement for you

David was the eight son of Jesse. He was in the field with his father's flock when Samuel came to anoint one of the Jesses king over Israel.

When Prophet Samuel took the horn of oil to on Eliab Jesse, the Lord stopped him. There was a divine rearrangement. Neither Abinadab, Shammah nor the rest siblings received the oil. David was ushered in from the field for the prophet would not sit down until all the sons of Jesse passed through his scrutiny.

By divine rearrangement and orchestration, David was anointed by Prophet Samuel. He was the future king of Israel. When your greatness is in the offing, there will be divine rearrangements. Things will fall in place, line upon line. You will blaze forth from obscurity to meteoric prominence.

You will get divine attention

You will get divine attention when your greatness is here. Blind Bartimaeus the son of Timaeus gained divine attention when it was time for him to receive his sight. The voices of opposition could not hinder him. The Bible says Jesus stood still and sent for him. He received his sight afterwards.

You will experience divine attention because your time for greatness has come! You will be sought for. You will be celebrated where you were tolerated. You will be a cynosure; a centre of attraction. You will become a beacon of light; a city set on a hill; the salt of the earth. You will be a render of last resort, an indispensable personality and an irresistible icon. Your name will ring bell. You will owe the ace. Your presence will be in high demand.

You will have answers to prayers

God answered the prayer of Hannah in Shiloh. It was her turn to be celebrated. Her several years of waiting was over. Samuel came as answer to her desire for greatness. Jabez prayed to have his coast enlarged. He had experience enough shame and ridicule in his growing years. God heard and answered his prayers and made him great.

'And Jabez called on the God of Israel, saying, Oh that thou wouldest bless me indeed, and enlarge my coast, and that thine hand might be with me, and that thou wouldest keep me from evil, that it may not grieve me! And God granted him that which he requested'- 1 Chron. 4:10

Let me show you a scripture you must watch out to be fulfilled for you as you ascend the ladder of greatness: Isaiah 65:24:

'And it shall come to pass, that before they call, I will answer; and while they are yet speaking, I will hear'

Your prayer will be God's priority. He will hear and answer you speedily.

You will sing a new song

'I waited patiently for the LORD; and he inclined unto me, and heard my cry. He brought me up also out of an horrible pit, out of the miry clay, and set my feet upon a rock, and established my goings. And he hath put a new song in my mouth, even praise unto our God: many shall see it, and fear, and shall trust in the LORD'- Psalms 40:1-3

'When the LORD turned again the captivity of Zion, we were like them that dream. Then was our mouth filled with laughter, and our tongue with singing: then said they among the heathen, The LORD hath done great things for them'- Psalms 126:1-2

Your greatness is here! Get ready to sing a new song. Get ready to be a testimony. You will be elevated and celebrated. You will be an invaluable vessel in the hand of God. You will become a worthy ambassador of Christ! I commend you to the God of greatness who is able to make you great. May his countenance shine upon you. May He lift you up to higher heights and greater glory. In Jesus greatest name!

Printed in the United States
By Bookmasters